NOTE

1. All spoon measurements are level.

2. All eggs are sizes 3, 4, 5 (standard) unless otherwise stated.

3. All sugar is granulated unless otherwise stated.

4. Preparation times given are an average calculated during recipe testing.

5. Metric and imperial measurements have been calculated separately. Use one set of measurements only as they are not exact equivalents.

6. Cooking times may vary slightly depending on the individual oven. Dishes should be placed in the centre of the oven unless otherwise specified.

7. Always preheat the oven or grill to the specified temperature.

8. Spoon measures can be bought in both imperial and metric sizes to give accurate measurement of small quantities.

Sweet Temptation

Wendy Majerowicz & Patricia Bourne

TREASURE PRESS

Contents

INTRODUCTION 4-5
BASIC PASTRIES 6-11
CONTINENTAL SPECIALITIES 12-25
TEATIME PASTRIES 26-35
PASTRY SAVOURIES 36-45
PIES AND FLANS 46-55
PETITS FOURS 56-65
CONFECTIONERY 66-79
INDEX 80

**First Printed in Great Britain in 1982 by
Octopus Books Limited**

This edition published in Great Britain in 1989 by
Treasure Press
Michelin House
81 Fulham Road
London SW3 6RB

© 1982 Hennerwood Publications Limited

ISBN 1 85051 401 1

Produced by Mandarin Offset
Printed and bound in Hong Kong

INTRODUCTION

Pastry making gives a great sense of achievement, and nothing can compare with the crisp perfection of home-made pastry. In the following pages, you will find all that you need to know about pastry making, together with a wide selection of traditional and original pies, tarts and flans. Even the more advanced pastries such as choux or puff pastry will quickly be mastered, and the most inexperienced cook will be able to produce mouthwatering dishes.

The chapter on sweet-making will provide both the experienced sweetmaker and the novice with ideas for satisfying results, and wet afternoons can be spent profitably making sweets to please all the family. Most faults in pastry making are easy to identify, so if success has eluded you in the past, or if your first attempts do not satisfy you, read the fault-finding guide on page 11, then try again. With practice you will soon be successful. When making and baking pastries, there are a few general points to bear in mind. Always keep pastries cool, using fingertips for rubbing in and handling, not the palms of the hands. If you have hot hands, run cold water over your wrists before starting to make the pastry. Make certain that boards, bowls and equipment are cool. Avoid making pastry in a hot kitchen, try to make it at the coolest time of day, or before the oven is lit. Roll out pastry with a light but firm action, always rolling away from you, not backwards and forwards.

Some recipes for flans tell you to 'bake blind'. This means to bake without a filling so that a crisp pastry case is ready to be filled with a variety of cream or fruit mixtures. To make certain the empty case has a good shape, line the flan tin without stretching the pastry, taking care that the pastry fits snugly into the tin where the base and sides meet.

Prick the base lightly to prevent it rising. Mould a crumpled piece of greaseproof paper against the inside of the pastry and fill with baking beans, piling them against the side of the pastry. Continue as directed in the individual recipe. Always make certain that the pastry is cooked at the right temperature, the shelf above the middle of the oven is the one to use for correct temperatures. Only an electric fan-assisted oven has even heat at all levels. Light the oven and set it to the correct temperature 15 minutes before you put the pastry in to cook. Many failures in pastry making are due to the oven not being at the right temperature at the start of the cooking time.

Equipment

Little special equipment is needed for making the pastries in this book. Although the best results will be obtained by using the sizes of tins given in the recipes, slightly smaller or larger ones can be used but the

cooking time may have to be adjusted. A good strong baking sheet which will not distort in the heat of the oven will be a worthwhile investment. Flan rings are easy to use, just place them on a baking sheet and line them with pastry. They are also easy to remove from the pastry when it is cooked and the case can then be returned to the oven to enable the sides to colour. If you prefer to use a loose-bottomed tin, the simplest way to prevent a burned wrist when removing the cooked flan, is to place the base on a jug or basin and allow the outside ring to slide over it.

Many 'tins' nowadays are made in aluminium or are non-stick and these have the advantage of being rustproof. However, ordinary tins will last a lifetime without deterioration, if they are dried in the residual heat of the oven when the cooking has finished and the power supply turned off. Pies and flans in ceramic or glass dishes look attractive on the table but to make certain the pastry is well cooked underneath the base, preheat a baking sheet and place your dish on this when it goes in the oven to cook. Boat-shaped tins (barquettes) make very attractive tartlets, but if they are not available, round ones can be used instead.

A good pastry board is another asset, and probably the best to use is a marble slab, which is excellent for keeping pastry cool. You can often buy an offcut of marble quite cheaply from a local stone-mason. A board is not only easy to clean at the sink, it will also protect the work surface of your kitchen units. Plastic laminates are easily scratched and damaged if a knife or cutter is used on them.

Storage

When storing pastries keep them in an airtight container. Flaky and puff pastries are best eaten on the day they are made, otherwise they should be reheated before eating. Put them into a preheated moderately hot oven for 5–7 minutes. If, like Cream Horns, they are to be filled, allow them to become completely cold before filling. Store empty cases carefully, as cooked pastry breaks easily.

Most sweets must be kept in absolutely airtight containers. Use waxed paper for separating layers of sweets such as peppermint creams and truffles. Sweets such as toffees, fudge and nougat will keep much better if each piece is wrapped in a small square of waxed paper.

Advance preparation

The recipes in this book have been selected to include a number of traditional favourites in every chapter, as well as a variety of new ones to try. Many of the pastry-based dishes have the advantage of being able to be made up either partly or entirely in advance – sometimes even the day before. Every recipe gives a useful indication of how long it will keep for, and where appropriate, how long the pastry base alone will store for.

Basic pastries

Crisp, light pastries are always great favourites. The following recipes will tell you clearly and explicitly, how to make all the pastries used in this book. The 'at-a-glance' charts will enable you to see immediately the amounts of the ingredients required for each quantity of pastry.

Remember that when a recipe calls for 100 g/4 oz pastry it means pastry made with that amount of flour. However, if instead, you choose to buy frozen pastry the amount stated on the packet is the total weight of the made pastry.

Lining a flan ring

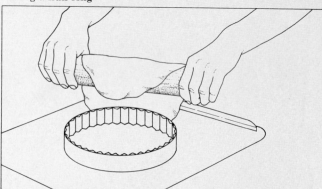

Lift the rolled out pastry into the tin, using a rolling pin

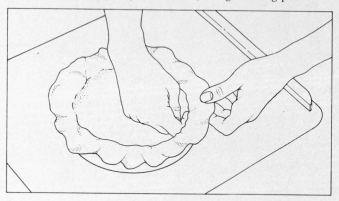

Press the pastry into the sides of the tin firmly but carefully

Roll off the excess pastry, using a rolling pin

Shortcrust pastry

Shortcrust pastry should be light and crisp with a delicately tinted colour. As it is quick to make and easy to shape and bake, it is frequently made into pies and tarts, pastries, turnovers and tartlets.

The ingredients are simple – about half the weight of fat to flour, a little salt and a measured amount of cold water. Half butter or margarine and half lard or other white fat is the usual combination of fats; this gives the colour and flavour of the butter or margarine and the short crisp texture which is characteristic of the white fat. Plain flour is used as a rule, though some people enjoy the rather cake-like texture which results from using self-raising flour, and this does make pleasant tartlet cases to fill with jam or lemon curd.

METRIC				IMPERIAL		
flour	100 g	175 g	225 g	4 oz	6 oz	8 oz
salt	pinch	pinch	1 × 1.25 ml spoon	pinch	pinch	$\frac{1}{4}$ teaspoon
butter or hard margarine	25 g	40 g	50 g	1 oz	$1\frac{1}{2}$ oz	2 oz
lard or white fat	25 g	40 g	50 g	1 oz	$1\frac{1}{2}$ oz	2 oz
water	1 × 15 ml spoon	$1\frac{1}{2}$ × 15 ml spoon	$2\frac{1}{2}$ × 15 ml spoon	1 tbs	$1\frac{1}{2}$ tbs	$2\frac{1}{2}$ tbs

Preparation time: 10 minutes
Oven: 200°C, 400°F, Gas Mark 6

Sift the flour and salt into a bowl. Add the fats and, using a round ended knife or palette knife, chop finely. Rub the fat into the flour with the fingertips. As the pastry is best kept cool, do not use the warm palms of your hands to rub in the fat.

When the mixture looks sufficiently fine, shake the bowl to bring any remaining lumps of fat to the surface and rub them in. The mixture should resemble fine breadcrumbs. Add the cold water and mix, first using a round ended knife and then the fingertips, to bind the pastry together to a ball of dough. A little more water can be added if necessary but a wet dough makes a tough pastry.

Knead the dough lightly on a floured board. The pastry can be used immediately or wrapped in cling film and kept in a cool place for a short time.

Wholemeal shortcrust pastry
Wholemeal flour can also be used to make the pastry for certain dishes. It gives an interesting change of flavour and texture and also adds fibre to the diet. Wholemeal shortcrust is made in the same way as shortcrust pastry except that wholemeal flour needs a little more water to bind the pastry together.

Cheese pastry

Cheese pastry can be used for all types of savoury tartlets and canapés. For small items such as these and cheese straws it needs no egg or water to bind and will be delightfully short in texture. If using for larger flans, cheese pastry will be easier to handle if a little water or egg yolk is added. Use finely grated Cheddar or similar hard cheese. If a stronger flavour is wanted, use half Cheddar and half Parmesan cheese.

METRIC					IMPERIAL
plain flour	100 g	175 g	225 g	4 oz	6 oz	8 oz
salt	pinch	good pinch	1 × 1.25 ml spoon	pinch	good pinch	$\frac{1}{4}$ teaspoon
paprika	pinch	good pinch	1 × 1.25 ml spoon	pinch	good pinch	$\frac{1}{4}$ teaspoon
butter	75 g	120 g	175 g	3 oz	$4\frac{1}{2}$ oz	6 oz
grated cheese	50 g	75 g	100 g	2 oz	3 oz	4 oz

Preparation time: 15 minutes

Sift the flour, salt and paprika into a bowl. Rub the butter into the flour, then add the grated cheese. Knead lightly together until the dough forms a smooth ball. If the dough is too soft to handle, chill for 20–30 minutes before using.

Pâte brisée (rich shortcrust pastry)

Use this pastry for flans and tarts with a moist filling. It has a firmer texture than shortcrust pastry and is therefore less likely to break. The traditional French way to make this pastry is on a board.

METRIC					IMPERIAL
plain flour	100 g	175 g	225 g	4 oz	6 oz	8 oz
caster sugar	15 g	20 g	25 g	$\frac{1}{2}$ oz	$\frac{3}{4}$ oz	1 oz
salt	pinch	pinch	1 × 1.25 ml spoon	pinch	pinch	$\frac{1}{4}$ teaspoon
butter	50 g	75 g	100 g	2 oz	3 oz	4 oz
egg	1 yolk	1 yolk	1	1 yolk	1 yolk	1
water or egg white	2 × 5 ml spoons	4 × 5 ml spoons	none	2 teaspoons	4 teaspoons	none

Preparation time: 15 minutes

Sift the flour, sugar and salt on to a board or into a bowl, make a well in the centre and add the butter, egg and water or egg white. Work in the flour until the mixture forms a ball. Knead lightly until smooth, do not overhandle or it will become tough. When ready wrap the pastry in cling film or greaseproof paper and chill in the refrigerator for 20–30 minutes before using.

Pâte Brisée can also be made quickly in an electric mixer or food processor in the same way as Pâte Sucrée (see page 8).

Pâte sucrée

Pâte Sucrée is a crisp sweet pastry ideal for flans and tartlets. It has a higher proportion of butter than most of the pastries which are used for these dishes. For best results, leave the butter at room temperature for several hours before using – it should be soft but not oily. Like Pâte Brisée, it should be made directly on a board, but can also be made in a bowl.

METRIC			IMPERIAL	
plain flour	65 g	150 g	$2\frac{1}{2}$ oz	5 oz
egg yolks	I	2	I	2
caster sugar	25 g	50 g	I oz	2 oz
butter	40 g	75 g	$1\frac{1}{2}$ oz	3 oz

Preparation time: 15 minutes

Sift the flour on to a board or into a bowl, make a well in the centre and add the egg yolks, caster sugar and butter. With the fingers of one hand, mix the egg yolks with the sugar and butter and gradually mix in the flour with both hands until it is all incorporated and the mixture has a crumbly appearance. Continue blending until a soft smooth ball of dough is formed. Because this pastry needs so much handling to incorporate the butter, wrap it in cling film or greaseproof paper and allow to rest in the refrigerator for 20–30 minutes, or until it becomes quite firm. Pâte Sucrée can also be made quickly in an electric mixer or food processor. Put all the ingredients into the bowl. Switch on the machine until the ingredients are completely mixed, then knead by hand until the pastry is completely smooth. If the speed is variable, use a low one.

Flaky pastry

The crisp featherlight layers of flaky pastry are always much admired and enjoyed. Although instructions for making it sound complex, it is really quite simple to make once you have mastered the basic technique. For the best results use a strong flour, the kind sold for breadmaking, though this is not essential. For a pastry with a good flavour and texture, use half butter or margarine and half lard. The consistency of the dough is important – it must be much softer than shortcrust pastry but not sticky. Some of the fat is rubbed in, but the remainder is added as the pastry is rolled and folded into layers. Air is trapped between the layers and this also makes the pastry rise.

Keep the pastry cool throughout the preparation so that it is easy to handle. When the cold pastry is put into the very hot oven the sudden heat makes it rise quickly. Do not open the oven door too soon; let the pastry cook for two-thirds of the expected cooking time before opening the oven door to look in.

METRIC				IMPERIAL		
plain flour	100 g	175 g	225 g	4 oz	6 oz	8 oz
salt	pinch	pinch	I × 1.25 ml spoon	pinch	pinch	$\frac{1}{4}$ tea-spoon
butter or margarine	40 g	50 g	75 g	$1\frac{1}{2}$ oz	2 oz	3 oz
lard or white fat	40 g	50 g	75 g	$1\frac{1}{2}$ oz	2 oz	3 oz
water	5 × 15 ml spoons	$7\frac{1}{2}$ × 15 ml spoons	150 ml	5 tbs	$7\frac{1}{2}$ tbs	$\frac{1}{4}$ pint

Preparation time: 20 minutes, plus relaxing
Oven: 200°C, 400°F, Gas Mark 6 or
       220°C, 425°F, Gas Mark 7

Sift the flour and salt into a bowl. Add half the butter or margarine and, using a round ended knife or palette knife, chop finely. Rub the fat into the flour with the fingertips. Add the measured amount of cold water and work in lightly using the same knife. A little more water can be added if necessary to bind the dough together to a soft but not sticky consistency.

Flour the pastry board lightly and shape the dough into a rectangle. Roll into a long oblong about 41 cm/16 inches long (if your pastry board is not this wide, turn it lengthwise on). Ease any rounded corners into shape. Mark lightly into thirds.

Using a round ended knife, dab half the lard in rough heaps on the top two-thirds of the pastry, leaving a border around the edge. Fold the lower third up over the centre section, then fold the top third down over this, keeping the corners square. Seal the edges with the rolling pin and give the pastry a half turn so that the fold is at the right hand side.

Roll the pastry out as before and repeat the process, first using the rest of the butter and then using the lard. Roll and fold once more without the addition of any more fat.

Wrap in cling film or put in a polythene container with a lid, and chill in the refrigerator for 20 minutes or longer before use. As the pastry needs to be cool all the time it is being made, it can be chilled between rollings during hot weather. Flaky pastry can be frozen if required.

Puff pastry

Puff pastry is the lightest and richest of all the pastries and rises in the most dramatic way. It is also the most difficult to make. Homemade puff pastry is unrivalled for taste and texture, however, ready made puff pastries can be purchased and these rise well too.

Use puff pastry for a light, crisp, well risen end result, as in Bouchées, Gâteau Jalousie aux Pommes or Almond Dartois.

The secret of successful puff pastry lies in making the dough soft enough to be elastic, but not so wet that it becomes soft and sticky. Care must be taken when rolling out the pastry to keep it even in shape, as poor layering gives an uneven rise. The pastry needs to be kept cool all the time, so use iced water to mix if the kitchen is warm and handle it as little as possible. Butter, rather than margarine, should be used, as the flavour is important to the taste of the pastry. Always keep the butter chilled in the refrigerator until it is needed.

For a well risen pastry, the oven must be correctly preheated and really hot when the cold pastry is put in so that the sudden heat makes it rise into light, flaky layers. The baking sheet need not be greased as the pastry contains so much fat; instead, damp it with a little cold water, this turns to steam and helps the pastry to rise well. A breadmaking flour gives elasticity to the dough and also helps to make a pastry that rises well.

Preparation time: 40 minutes, plus relaxing

Sift the flour and salt into a bowl, make a well in the centre and pour in half the water. Mix in a little of the flour from the sides of the bowl to the consistency of a white sauce, then using the fingertips lightly flake this paste through the flour. Sprinkle in half the remaining water, mix lightly again and continue in this way until the dough clings together without pressure. It should be a soft but not sticky dough; it may need a fraction more or less water depending on the flour. Wrap in cling film or put in a polythene container with a lid and chill in the refrigerator for at least 20 minutes. Place the chilled butter on a well floured board. Cover with a piece of butter paper or greaseproof paper and soften the butter by hitting it repeatedly with a rolling pin reducing it to half the thickness. Cut in half and put one piece on top of the other and repeat the process until the butter is about the same consistency as the dough.

Unwrap the dough and roll out on a floured board to the size of a large dinner plate. Place the butter in the centre and wrap the dough over from each side. Seal lightly with the rolling pin then fold the ends of the dough into the centre. At this point, it is often more convenient to turn the board around so that the length is towards you.

Give the pastry a half turn sideways and roll to a long strip about the length of the board, keeping the edges straight and the ends square. Fold in thirds as for Flaky Pastry (opposite), give a half turn sideways ready to roll and fold again. Wrap as before and refrigerate for 20 minutes.

Repeat the rolling and folding 4 times, putting the pastry to chill after 2 rollings and foldings. Wrap and chill for at least 20 minutes before using. It is often convenient to make the puff pastry dough the day before it is needed, or it can be frozen.

METRIC				IMPERIAL		
plain flour	100 g	175 g	225 g	4 oz	6 oz	8 oz
salt	pinch	pinch	1×2.5 ml	pinch	pinch	$\frac{1}{4}$ teaspoon
water	5×15 ml spoons	$7\frac{1}{2} \times 15$ ml spoons	150 ml	5 tbs	$7\frac{1}{2}$ tbs	$\frac{1}{4}$ pint
chilled butter	100 g	175 g	225 g	4 oz	6 oz	8 oz

Choux pastry

Choux pastry has many uses, both sweet and savoury. For success in making it, first of all, weigh and measure accurately. Make certain that the butter has melted before the water starts to boil, and the water must be boiling when the flour is added. Be careful not to open the oven door until at least three-quarters of the cooking time has elapsed.

METRIC				IMPERIAL		
water	150 ml	225 ml	300 ml	$\frac{1}{4}$ pint	$7\frac{1}{2}$ fl oz	$\frac{1}{2}$ pint
butter	50 g	75 g	100 g	2 oz	3 oz	4 oz
strong flour	65 g	95 g	150 g	$2\frac{1}{2}$ oz	$3\frac{3}{4}$ oz	5 oz
eggs	2	3	4	2	3	4

Preparation time: 20 minutes

Oven: 220°C, 425°F, Gas Mark 7;
190°C, 375°F, Gas Mark 5

Put the water and butter in a saucepan over a low heat until the butter has melted, then raise the heat until the water boils and rises in the pan. Immediately add the sifted flour and beat well over the heat until the mixture leaves the side of the pan and forms a smooth ball. Remove from the heat and leave to cool for a few minutes.

Beat the eggs lightly and add them to the mixture a little at a time. Beat each addition of egg in well until the mixture regains its original stiff consistency.

An electric mixer can be used at this stage, but if an aluminium pan is used it is essential to transfer the mixture to a bowl before adding the eggs because the action of the beaters on the saucepan could discolour the mixture.

Choux pastry should be cooked in a hot oven for the first 10 minutes so that it rises rapidly. The temperature is then reduced for the remainder of the cooking time. Pierce choux buns and éclairs on the base or side when they are cooked to allow the steam to escape. If necessary, return to the oven for a few minutes to dry them out. For the best results, cook one tray at a time. Choux pastry can also be deep fried for Aigrettes au Fromage, fritters etc.

Using Choux Pastry and Pâte Sucrée to make Polkas (page 21)

Fault finding guide

FAULT	Causes & Solutions
RUBBED IN PASTRIES – Shortcrust, pâte brisée (rich shortcrust), wholemeal, cheese, and pâte sucrée.	
Crumbly dough	Insufficient mixing. Knead lightly to form a ball. Not enough liquid. Add more, a few drops at a time.
Sticky dough	Too much liquid. Add a little more flour. Flour not weighed accurately. Pâte sucrée, pâte brisée (rich shortcrust) and cheese pastry not chilled before rolling.
Cooked pastry hard and tough	Too much water worked in. Over-handled. Rolled out in too much flour. Flour sprinkled over pastry during rolling.
Cooked pastry soft and crumbly	Too much fat used. Too little liquid added. Self-raising flour used for pâte brisée (rich shortcrust) and pâte sucrée.
Pastry shrunk	Stretched during lifting or shaping. Pâte brisée (rich shortcrust) and pâte sucrée not allowed to relax before using. Pastry cooked in too cool oven.
Pastry covering pie has sunk	Oven temperature too cool. Insufficient filling to pie. Pastry put over a hot filling.
Flan sides collapsed	Oven temperature too low. Insufficient baking beans used, or they were not piled up against sides of flan.
Soft under-cooked pastry	Oven temperature too low. Oven not properly preheated. Baking sheet not used under a flan tin. Too much liquid used in a pie. Top of pie or turnover not slit to allow the steam to escape.
FLAKY PASTRY AND PUFF PASTRY	
Sticky dough	Flour incorrectly weighed. Too much water added. Add a little more flour before rolling out. Dough not chilled enough.
Pastry not risen	Fat not cool enough. Dough too tight; insufficient water added

FAULT	Causes & Solutions
FLAKY AND PUFF PASTRY CONTINUED	Insufficient resting and chilling. Over-heavy rolling.
Uneven rising	Poor folding – corners must be eased out and pastry folded neatly into 3 layers. Uneven rolling.
Fat breaking through the dough	Fat too hard so that it breaks through when rolling. Insufficient chilling. Over-handling. Over-heavy rolling.
Fat running out during cooking	Fat broke through the dough while making (see above). Oven temperature too low.
Pastry hard and tough	Too much water or too little water added to dough – it should be soft but not sticky.
Pastry shrinking	Insufficient resting. Pastry stretched during cutting, shaping or lifting.
Damp and soggy inside	Insufficiently cooked. Bouchées not put back into the oven to dry after the insides have been removed.
CHOUX PASTRY	
Mixture too soft	Wrong proportions of ingredients used – weigh and measure accurately. Water not boiling when flour added. Mixture not cooked until it leaves sides of pan. Too much egg added at once. Insufficient beating when each amount of egg is added.
Mixture not risen	Wrong proportions of ingredients used. Mixture too soft. Mixture not beaten enough. Oven too cool. Temperature lowered too soon. Oven doors opened during cooking Not cooked long enough.
Sinking when removed from oven	Not cooked long enough – return to the oven quickly.
Soft and soggy inside	Bases not pricked to allow the steam to escape. Not returned to oven after pricking to dry.

CONTINENTAL SPECIALITIES

Every country in Europe has its own
specialities and there are countless variations
in the ingredients and presentation of each
one. From Austria we enjoy the delicate
crispness of a well baked strudel and France
has an indefinite variety of fruit flans.
Some of these recipes take careful preparation,
but are well worth the effort.
To save time, when you have to cater for a
party, make large size flans and gâteaux – they
take little longer to prepare than small ones.

Tartelettes aux fruits; Crème patissière (on the right)

Crème patissière (confectioner's custard)

Metric	Imperial
300 ml milk	½ pint milk
1 vanilla pod	1 vanilla pod
1 egg	1 egg
1 egg yolk	1 egg yolk
50 g caster sugar, sifted	2 oz caster sugar, sifted
25 g plain flour, sifted	1 oz plain flour, sifted

Preparation time: 10 minutes
Cooking time: 45 minutes

Place the milk and the vanilla pod in a saucepan. Bring just to the boil, remove from the heat and leave for 20–30 minutes.
Put the egg and egg yolk into a bowl with the sugar. Beat well together, until creamy, then add the flour and mix until smooth. Remove the vanilla pod from the milk, wash and dry it.
Reheat the milk until just below boiling, then pour it on to the egg mixture. Stir well until blended together, then return to the saucepan and place over a gentle heat. Bring to the boil, stirring continuously. If the mixture forms any lumps, beat well until smooth. Simmer for a further 2–3 minutes, stirring continuously. Leave to cool before using.
Use on the same day.
Makes 300 ml/½ pint

Variation:

Substitute 1–2 drops vanilla essence instead of the vanilla pod, but it will not have such a good flavour. Add the essence after the custard is cooked.

Tartelettes aux fruits

Metric	Imperial
65 g Pâte Sucrée (page 8)	2½ oz Pâte Sucrée (page 8)
100 g plain chocolate	4 oz plain chocolate
5 × 15 ml spoons apricot jam or redcurrant jelly (see method)	5 tablespoons apricot jam or redcurrant jelly (see method)
50 g almonds, finely chopped and toasted	2 oz almonds, finely chopped and toasted
150 ml cold Crème Patissière	¼ pint cold Crème Patissière
225 g fruit (see below)	8 oz fruit (see below)

Preparation time: 40–45 minutes
Cooking time: 10–15 minutes
Oven: 190°C, 375°F, Gas Mark 5

A variety of fruits can be used for these tartlets, either canned or fresh. Fresh raspberries and strawberries are delicious when in season. Fresh blackcurrants, redcurrants and gooseberries, and fruits such as apricots and peaches, must be poached in a syrup made with 300 ml/½ pint water and 75 g/3 oz sugar. Cook them gently so that they remain whole. When cooked, drain well and allow to cool. Peaches and apricots should be cut into slices. Canned mandarin orange segments and pineapple or other canned fruit can be used when fresh fruit is not available.

Roll out the pastry thinly and use to line twelve 10 cm/4 inch boat-shaped tartlet tins. Prick the pastry well, place in a preheated oven and bake for 10–12 minutes until a light golden brown. Remove from the tins and cool on a wire tray.
Melt the chocolate in a bowl over hot water. Brush the insides of the tartlet cases with the melted chocolate and leave to harden. Heat the jam or jelly, using apricot jam for yellow and orange fruit and redcurrant jelly for the others. Brush the edge of each tartlet and dip into the finely chopped almonds.
Spread a little of the Crème Patissière in the bottom of each tartlet and arrange the fruit neatly on top. Brush the fruit with the jam or jelly glaze. Serve cold.
  Empty cases keep up to 7 days in an airtight container. When filled, eat on the same day.
Makes 12

Linzer torte

Preparation time: 45 minutes, plus chilling
Cooking time: 50 minutes
Oven: 200°C, 400°F, Gas Mark 6

Metric	*Imperial*
100 g ground unblanched hazelnuts	*4 oz ground unblanched hazelnuts*
100 g plain flour, sifted	*4 oz plain flour, sifted*
100 g caster sugar	*4 oz caster sugar*
100 g butter	*4 oz butter*
2 egg yolks	*2 egg yolks*
450 g raspberry jam	*1 lb raspberry jam*
1 egg, beaten	*1 egg, beaten*
icing sugar, to finish	*icing sugar, to finish*

Place the ground hazelnuts, flour and caster sugar into a bowl and mix well. Add the butter and rub in with the fingertips as for Shortcrust Pastry (page 6). Add the egg yolks and work the pastry until it forms a smooth ball. Chill for at least 30 minutes before using. Roll out three-quarters of the pastry to 5 mm/¼ inch thick and use to line an 18 cm/7 inch flan ring. Trim the edge. Fill the centre with the jam.

Knead the trimmings and the remaining pastry to a smooth ball and roll out into a circle slightly wider than the flan ring and 5 mm/¼ inch thick. Cut into thin strips and arrange a neat lattice pattern on the top of the jam. Trim the edge and brush the pastry with beaten egg.

Place in a preheated oven and bake for about 1 hour until the pastry is golden brown and firm. Leave in the flan case on the baking sheet until nearly cold, otherwise the tart will be difficult to handle. Sift icing sugar evenly over the top before serving.

Keeps up to 4 days.
Serves 6–8

Apple and apricot strudel

Metric
225 g plain flour
1 × 1.25 ml spoon salt
2 × 15 ml cooking oil
1 × 2.5 ml spoon wine
   vinegar
1 egg
90 ml water

Filling:
175 g dried apricots,
   soaked overnight
175 g caster sugar
50 g unsalted butter
350 g cooking apples
75 g fresh white
   breadcrumbs
1 × 5 ml spoon ground
   cinnamon
50 g butter, melted
50 g ground almonds
little icing sugar, to finish

Imperial
8 oz plain flour
¼ teaspoon salt
2 tablespoons cooking oil
½ tablespoon wine
   vinegar
1 egg
3 fl oz water

Filling:
6 oz dried apricots,
   soaked overnight
6 oz caster sugar
2 oz unsalted butter
12 oz cooking apples
3 oz fresh white
   breadcrumbs
1 teaspoon ground
   cinnamon
2 oz butter, melted
2 oz ground almonds
little icing sugar, to finish

Preparation time: 50 minutes, plus soaking
and chilling
Cooking time: 45 minutes
Oven: 220°C, 425°F, Gas Mark 7;
   190°C, 375°F, Gas Mark 5

Strudels must be the most popular of all the Viennese pastries. Apple Strudel is encountered most often, but other fillings are also excellent and this one, with apricots, is typical and delicious. The pastry must be rolled *very* thinly until it is almost transparent so that it is light and flaky to eat.

Sift the flour and salt into a bowl, make a well in the centre and pour in the oil, vinegar, egg and water. Stir the flour into the liquid and mix to a soft dough. Knead this well, first in the bowl and then on a lightly floured board; it should be soft and springy. Put in a polythene container with a lid or wrap in cling film and place in the refrigerator for 1 hour or overnight. Drain the apricots, put in a saucepan with 50 g/2 oz of the sugar and 150 ml/¼ pint water and simmer until tender. Leave to cool. When cold, drain and chop. Heat the butter in a frying pan, add the breadcrumbs and fry until golden brown. Drain on paper towels and leave to cool. Peel and core the apples, slice very thinly. Mix the rest of the sugar and cinnamon together.
Put a clean, well-ironed teatowel or small tablecloth on a working surface and sprinkle it lightly with flour. Roll out the chilled pastry on this until it is very thin, then continue to make the pastry into an even thinner sheet by easing it out gently with the palms of your hands flat underneath it. (Tradition says that you should be able to read a love letter through the dough.) Take care not to tear the pastry. Trim the edges with scissors to remove the thick edge and neaten the shape. Leave on the cloth for 15 minutes – this dries the pastry a little so that it bakes better.
Brush the surface of the pastry with half the melted butter. Sprinkle with the fried breadcrumbs and the sugar, cinnamon and ground almonds, leaving a 2.5 cm/1 inch border all round. Cover with the apple slices and apricots. Moisten the edges of the pastry with water.
Take hold of the cloth at the edge nearest to you and gently lift it so that the pastry rolls over and over like a Swiss roll. Finish with the seam underneath. Place on a greased baking sheet and shape into a horseshoe. Brush with the remaining melted butter. Place in a preheated oven and bake for 20 minutes. Reduce the oven temperature and cook for a further 25 minutes. Cool on a wire tray. Dredge with icing sugar.
Best eaten on the same day, but can be used next day.
Serves 8

Linzer torte; Apple and apricot strudel

Tarte frangipane

Metric
50 g glacé cherries, chopped
1 × 15 ml spoon lemon juice
150 g Pâte Sucrée (page 8)

Imperial
2 oz glacé cherries, chopped
1 tablespoon lemon juice
5 oz Pâte Sucrée (page 8)

Filling:
100 g butter
100 g caster sugar
2 eggs, lightly beaten
25 g plain flour
100 g ground almonds
1 × 15 ml spoon rum

Filling:
4 oz butter
4 oz caster sugar
2 eggs, lightly beaten
1 oz plain flour
4 oz ground almonds
1 tablespoon rum

To decorate:
25 g icing sugar, sifted
25 g almonds, blanched and sliced
few glacé cherries, halved
crystallized angelica

To decorate:
1 oz icing sugar, sifted
1 oz almonds, blanched and sliced
few glacé cherries, halved
crystallized angelica

Preparation time: 40 minutes
Cooking time: 40 minutes
Oven: 180°C, 350°F, Gas Mark 4

There are many variations of this traditional almond and cherry flan. It freezes well, but as the flavour of rum is lost in freezing, substitute this with lemon juice, and decorate the flan after defrosting with the icing mixed with a little rum instead of water.

Macerate the glacé cherries in the lemon juice.
Roll out the pastry into a circle, turning it frequently to prevent sticking, and use to line a 23 cm/9 inch flan ring. Prick the base lightly.
Cream the butter and sugar together until light and fluffy. Add the egg, a little at a time. Sift the flour and ground almonds together and fold into the creamed mixture, half at a time, with the rum.
Spread the cherries over the bottom of the flan case and cover evenly with the almond mixture. Place in a preheated oven and bake for about 40 minutes until set and golden brown. Remove the flan tin and cool on a wire tray.
Meanwhile, blend the icing sugar with a little water to make a thin icing. Spread this thinly over the top of the tart and sprinkle with the almonds, allow to set and brush with more icing. Decorate with the glacé cherries and angelica.
Keeps up to 4 days.
Serves 6–8

Tarte aux abricots bourdaloue

Metric
150 g Pâte Sucrée (page 8)

Imperial
5 oz Pâte Sucrée (page 8)

Filling:
300 ml milk
1 vanilla pod or few drops of vanilla essence
40 g sugar
2 egg yolks
25 g ground rice
25 g ground almonds
15 g butter
1 × 15 ml spoon Kirsch or few drops of almond essence
1 × 400 g can apricot halves, drained
3 × 15 ml spoons sieved apricot jam

Filling:
½ pint milk
1 vanilla pod or few drops of vanilla essence
1½ oz sugar
2 egg yolks
1 oz ground rice
1 oz ground almonds
½ oz butter
1 tablespoon Kirsch or few drops of almond essence
1 × 14 oz can apricot halves, drained
3 tablespoons sieved apricot jam

Preparation time: 40 minutes
Cooking time: 25 minutes
Oven: 190°C, 375°F, Gas Mark 5

Roll out the pastry into a circle and use to line an 18 cm/7 inch flan ring or dish. Prick the base well. Line the flan with greaseproof paper and beans, place in a preheated oven and bake blind for 20 minutes until pale gold. Remove the paper and beans, and return the flan to the oven for 5 minutes to dry the base. Remove the flan ring and cool on a wire tray.
For the filling, warm the milk with the vanilla pod and leave to stand for 30 minutes to infuse the flavour. Alternatively, warm the milk, then add the vanilla essence, if using.
Put the sugar, egg yolks, ground rice and ground almonds into a bowl and stir together. Remove the vanilla pod from the milk.
Pour the warm milk on to the egg yolk mixture, stir well and return to the heat. Bring slowly to the boil, stirring continuously, and cook for 4–5 minutes. Remove from the heat and stir in the butter and Kirsch or almond essence. Pour into a bowl and put a piece of cling film or damp greaseproof paper on the top surface to stop a skin forming.
When the filling is cool, remove the covering and pour into the flan case. Arrange the halved apricots to cover the cream filling. Boil the apricot glaze and brush this over the top and sides of the flan.
Empty case keeps up to 4 days in an airtight tin. When filled, eat on the same day.
Serves 4–6

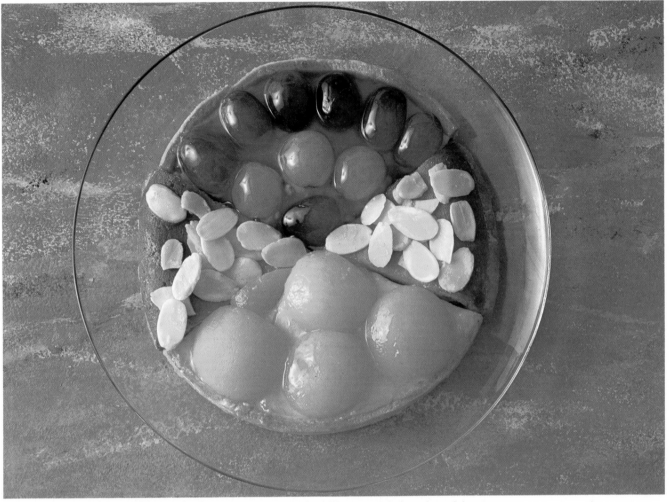

Top: Tarte aux raisins; left and right: Tarte frangipane; below: Tarte aux abricots bourdaloue

Tarte aux raisins

Metric
150 g Pâte Sucrée (page
   8)
300 ml cold Crème
   Patissière (page 13)

Imperial
5 oz Pâte Sucrée (page
   8)
½ pint cold Crème
   Patissière (page 13)

To decorate:
100 g white grapes,
   halved and seeded
100 g black grapes,
   halved and seeded
3 × 15 ml spoons
   redcurrant jelly

To decorate:
4 oz white grapes, halved
   and seeded
4 oz black grapes, halved
   and seeded
3 tablespoons redcurrant
   jelly

Preparation time: 50 minutes
Cooking time: 25 minutes
Oven: 190°C, 375°F, Gas Mark 5

Autumn is a specially good time to make this flan,
when grapes are ripe and full flavoured. In sum-
mertime adapt the recipe to the season, using strawberries or raspberries in place of the grapes.

Roll out the pastry into a circle and use to line an 18
cm/7 inch flan ring. Bake blind in a preheated oven for
20 minutes. Remove the greaseproof paper and
baking beans and return to the oven for 5 minutes.
Remove the flan ring and cool on a wire tray.
When the pastry is cold, whisk the custard well and
pour into the flan case. Decorate the top with alternate
circles of black and white grapes.
Put the redcurrant jelly in a saucepan and bring to the
boil, whisking until smooth. Brush the fruit with the
hot redcurrant jelly. Allow to cool then place on a
serving plate.
Empty case keeps up to 4 days in an airtight tin. When
filled, eat on the same day.
Serves 4–6

Tarte aux cerises alsacienne

Metric
450 g cherries
100 g Pâte Brisée (page 7)
50 g plain flour
50 g caster sugar
150 ml double or whipping cream
little caster sugar, to finish

Imperial
1 lb cherries
4 oz Pâte Brisée (page 7)
2 oz plain flour
2 oz caster sugar
¼ pint double or whipping cream
little caster sugar, to finish

Preparation time: 20–30 minutes
Cooking time: 35–40 minutes
Oven: 190°C, 375°F, Gas Mark 5

The district of Alsace-Lorraine on the eastern border of France has had a turbulent history, sometimes being part of Germany and at others, as now, of France. This has given the food of the region a character of its own, but like the rest of France, it still makes full use of the best of its local products. Cherry orchards abound in this region and so it is natural that one of its traditional recipes should be a cherry tart.

Roll out the pastry and use to line an 18 cm/7 inch flan ring. Prick the base lightly. Stone the cherries and arrange them neatly on the base of the flan. Place in a preheated oven and bake for 10 minutes.
Meanwhile, mix the flour, sugar and cream together. Spread this mixture over the cherries, return to the oven and continue baking for a further 25–30 minutes. Remove from the flan ring and place on a wire tray. Sift a little caster sugar over the top and serve. Keeps up to 2 days in the refrigerator.
Serves 5–6

Tarte aux cerises alsacienne; Gâteau Saint Honoré

Gâteau Saint Honoré

Metric
65 g Pâte Sucrée (page 8)
95 g Choux Pastry (page 10)
1 egg, beaten

Crème St. Honoré
300 ml milk
1 vanilla pod
2 egg yolks
50 g caster sugar
50 g plain flour
5 egg whites

To finish:
175 g sugar
4 × 15 ml spoons water
glacé cherries, halved
crystallized angelica

Imperial
2½ oz Pâte Sucrée (page 8)
3¾ oz Choux Pastry (page 10)
1 egg, beaten

Crème St. Honoré
½ pint milk
1 vanilla pod
2 egg yolks
1 oz caster sugar
2 oz plain flour
5 egg whites

To finish:
6 oz sugar
4 tablespoons water
glacé cherries, halved
crystallized angelica

Preparation time: 30–40 minutes
Cooking time: 30–40 minutes
Oven: 220°C, 425°F, Gas Mark 7;
190°C, 375°F, Gas Mark 5

This gâteau is named after Saint Honoré who is the Patron Saint of pastry cooks. The filling is called Crème Saint Honoré and can be used to fill other gâteaux such as Paris-Brest. Eat this gâteau the same day that it is made, preferably within 3–4 hours of making.

Roll out the pastry into a 20 cm/8 inch circle, using a saucepan lid or dessert plate as a guide. Place on a baking sheet and prick the pastry well.
Put the choux pastry into a piping bag fitted with a 1 cm/½ inch plain nozzle. Brush around the outside edge of the Pâte Sucrée with the beaten egg and pipe a band of choux pastry on top of this. Pipe the rest of the choux pastry into small balls on to a greased baking sheet.
Brush the top of all the choux pastry with beaten egg. Cover the Pâte Sucrée in the centre with a circle of greaseproof paper. Place in a preheated oven and bake for 10 minutes. Reduce the oven temperature and continue cooking for a further 20–30 minutes until the choux pastry is crisp and golden brown. If the Pâte Sucrée colours too much, lower the oven temperature slightly for the last 10 minutes of baking time.
Remove from the oven, take the greaseproof paper from the centre and cool on a wire tray. Using a skewer, make a hole in the base of each choux ball and cool them on the wire tray.
Meanwhile, make the Crème St. Honoré. Place the milk and vanilla pod in a pan and bring just to the boil. Leave on one side for at least 30 minutes for the vanilla flavour to infuse the milk.
Cream the egg yolks, sugar and flour together. Reheat the milk and remove the vanilla pod. Pour the milk on to the mixture and mix well together. Return to the pan and bring to the boil, stirring continuously, until the mixture thickens. Boil for 2–3 minutes. Whisk the egg whites until they are stiff and fold them into the hot custard. (It is essential that the custard is very hot so that it sets the egg whites; so if necessary reheat the custard again.) Allow to cool, then spread in an even layer in the bottom of the gâteau case.
Dissolve the sugar in the water in a large pan. Bring to the boil and cook until the syrup turns a light golden brown. Remove from the heat. Using a skewer, dip the top of each choux ball into the caramel, taking care not to burn your fingers. Dip the base of each one into the caramel and arrange them on top of the choux pastry ring. Decorate with halved cherries and angelica leaves. Serve cold.
Eat on the same day.
Serves 6–8

Paris-Brest

Metric	Imperial
95 g Choux Pastry (page 10)	3¾ oz Choux Pastry (page 10)
1 egg, beaten	1 egg, beaten
25 g flaked almonds	1 oz flaked almonds

Filling:	Filling:
2 egg whites	2 egg whites
120 g icing sugar, sifted	4½ oz icing sugar, sifted
240 g unsalted butter, at room temperature	8½ oz unsalted butter, at room temperature
4 × 15 ml spoons coarsely crushed Praline (opposite)	4 tablespoons coarsely crushed Praline (opposite)
little icing sugar, to finish	little icing sugar, to finish

Preparation time: 40 minutes
Cooking time: 30–35 minutes
Oven: 220°C, 425°F, Gas Mark 7;
      190°C, 375°F, Gas Mark 5

This gâteau, named after the famous cycle race, is filled with a rich Crème au Beurre à la Meringue flavoured with praline. It can be served for teatime, buffet parties or dinner parties and is best eaten the day it is prepared. If left overnight, the crunchy texture of the praline in the filling is lost as the sugar coating dissolves.

Lightly grease a baking sheet. Place the choux pastry into a piping bag fitted with a large star nozzle and pipe a thick 20 cm/8 inch circle. Brush with the beaten egg and sprinkle the almonds over the top. Place in a preheated oven and bake for 10 minutes. Reduce the oven temperature and continue cooking for a further 20–25 minutes until the ring is golden brown and crisp. Remove from the oven, cut the ring in half, making 2 circles, and cool on a wire tray.
Meanwhile, make the filling. Put the egg whites and icing sugar into a large bowl and mix together. Place over a pan of hot water over a gentle heat and whisk until the mixture is stiff and stands in peaks. Remove from the heat and continue whisking until it is completely cold.
Cut the softened butter into small pieces. Whisk the butter into the meringue a piece at a time. Continue whisking until the mixture is smooth and then fold in the crushed praline. Place in a piping bag fitted with a 1 cm/½ inch nozzle and pipe into the bottom half of the pastry ring. Cover with the other pastry ring and sift icing sugar over the top.
Empty case keeps for 24 hours. When filled, eat on the same day.
Serves 6–8

Praline

Metric	Imperial
100 g unblanched almonds	4 oz unblanched almonds
100 g sugar	4 oz sugar
4 × 15 ml spoons water	4 tablespoons water

Preparation time: 10 minutes
Cooking time: 20 minutes

Wash the almonds in cold water to remove the powder which clings to the skins.
Place the sugar and water in a small heavy saucepan over a gentle heat and stir with a wooden spoon until the sugar has dissolved. Remove the spoon and do not stir again (see notes on sugar boiling on page 72).
Add the almonds to the syrup, bring to the boil and boil rapidly until it reaches extra hard crack stage, 175°C/350°F, and turns a rich brown colour.
Pour on to an oiled baking sheet which should be resting on a pot stand or board to protect the working surface from the heat. Allow to cool.
Crush in a pestle and mortar or with a rolling pin. If very fine praline is needed grind it in a liquidizer.
Keeps up to 6 weeks in an airtight tin.

Polkas

Metric	Imperial
65 g Pâte Sucrée (page 8)	2½ oz Pâte Sucrée (page 8)
65 g Choux Pastry (page 10)	2½ oz Choux Pastry (page 10)
100 g icing sugar	4 oz icing sugar
juice of ½ lemon	juice of ½ lemon
150 ml double or whipping cream, whipped	¼ pint double or whipping cream, whipped
225 g strawberries, hulled	8 oz strawberries, hulled
3 × 15 ml spoons redcurrant jelly	3 tablespoons redcurrant jelly

Preparation time: 35–45 minutes
Cooking time: 30–35 minutes
Oven: 220°C, 425°F, Gas Mark 7;
      190°C, 375°F, Gas Mark 5

Polkas are individual tartlets made like small Gâteau Saint Honoré and filled with fruit and cream. Small strawberries are best for these tartlets; but peaches and apricots can be substituted.

Roll out the Pâte Sucrée, cut into 7.5 cm/3 inch circles and place on a baking sheet.
Put the choux pastry into a piping bag fitted with a 1 cm/½ inch plain nozzle and pipe a ring of choux pastry just inside the edge of each circle. Place in a preheated oven and bake for 10 minutes. Reduce the oven temperature and continue cooking for a further 20–25 minutes until golden brown. Cool on a wire tray.
Sift the icing sugar into a shallow bowl and add the lemon juice and sufficient warm water to blend to a soft smooth icing. Hold each polka upside down and dip into the icing to coat the ring of choux pastry.
Pipe or spoon the whipped cream into the centre of each polka. Arrange the strawberries on top of the cream. Boil the redcurrant jelly, whisking until smooth, and brush over the top of the strawberries. Eat on the same day.
Makes 6–8

From the top: Polkas; Paris–Brest

Gâteau jalousie aux pommes

Metric	Imperial
450 g cooking apples, peeled and cored	1 lb cooking apples, peeled and cored
grated rind of 1 lemon	grated rind of 1 lemon
175 g sugar	6 oz sugar
225 g Puff Pastry (page 9), chilled	8 oz Puff Pastry (page 9), chilled
1 egg, beaten	1 egg, beaten
little icing sugar	little icing sugar

Preparation time: 50 minutes
Cooking time: 35 minutes
Oven: 220°C, 425°F, Gas Mark 7;
       190°C, 375°F, Gas Mark 5

Jalousie are the slatted window shutters that are to be seen on many French houses, especially in the hotter parts of the country. The top of this tart is decorated to look like one of these shutters, with the pastry cut into thin slats and the filling peeping through.

Cut the apples into chunks and put in a pan with the lemon rind and a little water. Cover and simmer gently for 15–20 minutes until the fruit is tender, and excess liquid evaporated. Rub through a sieve, add the sugar and reboil until a little thicker. Spread on a plate to cool.

Roll out the pastry to a 36 × 30 cm/14 × 12 inch rectangle. Trim the edges straight and cut in half lengthwise to give 2 pieces 36 × 15 cm/14 × 6 inches. Place 1 piece on a dampened baking sheet. Brush a 2.5 cm/1 inch border with beaten egg and put the cold apple purée down the centre.

Sprinkle the top of the second piece of pastry with flour and fold lengthwise. Cut straight slits on the folded edge 5 mm/¼ inch apart, leaving a 2.5 cm/1 inch border on the cut edge. Open out, and dust off the surplus flour with a dry pastry brush. Lift on to the base and put the edges together. Press firmly together, using the side of the hand, then knock up the edge. Place in a preheated oven and bake for 20 minutes. Sprinkle with icing sugar, reduce the oven temperature and continue cooking for another 15 minutes or until it has a shiny brown glaze. Cool on a wire tray.
Keeps up to 2 days.
Serves 6

Tarte de pommes à la normande

Metric	Imperial
75 g butter	3 oz butter
75 g caster sugar	3 oz caster sugar
1 egg, beaten	1 egg, beaten
75 g ground almonds	3 oz ground almonds
1½ × 15 ml spoons plain flour, sifted	1½ tablespoons plain flour, sifted
1 × 15 ml spoon Kirsch or rum	1 tablespoon Kirsch or rum
175 g Pâte Brisée (page 7)	6 oz Pâte Brisée (page 7)

To decorate:	To decorate:
3 medium apples	3 medium apples
little icing sugar	little icing sugar
apricot jam, sieved	apricot jam, sieved

Preparation time: 35 minutes
Cooking time: 35–40 minutes
Oven: 200°C, 400°F, Gas Mark 6;
       190°C, 375°F, Gas Mark 5

The apple orchards of Normandy inspire the cooks of the area to produce a variety of apple flans. This recipe, with an almond filling, is particularly attractive. Although in France it is usually served cold, it may also be served warm.

To make the filling, cream the butter and sugar together until light and fluffy. Beat in the eggs, a little at a time, then fold in the ground almonds, flour and Kirsch or rum.

Roll out the pastry into a circle and use to line a 23 cm/9 inch flan ring or china flan dish. Trim the edges, fill with the almond cream and smooth the surface. Peel, halve and core the apples. Cut each apple half across into slices. Keeping each cut apple half together, slide a knife under to lift and place on the flan, sliding the slices slightly apart. Press down into the cream filling.

Place in a preheated oven and bake for 15 minutes. Reduce the oven temperature and continue cooking for a further 10 minutes. Sprinkle with a little sifted icing sugar and return to the oven for about 10 minutes; the apples should be tender and the filling pleasantly coloured. Remove from the oven, take off the flan ring if used and cool on a wire tray.
Warm the apricot jam and add a little water if needed. Brush this glaze over the flan.
Keeps up to 2 days.
Serves 8

From the top: Gâteau jalousie aux pommes; Tarte de pommes à la normande

Tranche aux fruits

Metric	Imperial
175 g Puff Pastry (page 9), chilled or 1 × 375 g packet frozen puff pastry, thawed	6 oz Puff Pastry (page 9), chilled, or 1 × 13 oz packet frozen puff pastry, thawed
1 egg, beaten	1 egg, beaten
250 ml double or whipping cream, whipped	8 fl oz double or whipping cream, whipped
3 × 15 ml spoons apricot jam, sieved	3 tablespoons apricot jam, sieved
225 g strawberries, hulled	8 oz strawberries, hulled
2 × 15 ml spoons redcurrant jelly	2 tablespoons redcurrant jelly

Preparation time: 20 minutes, plus chilling
Cooking time: 20 minutes
Oven 230°C, 450°F, Gas Mark 8

Before you start, make sure your serving plate is large enough. Strawberries are excellent to use but other fruit such as grapes, orange segments, raspberries, or fresh or canned pineapple can be used. An attractive way to present it is with a selection of fruits arranged in lines of contrasting colours. Use redcurrant jelly for glazing red fruits, otherwise use apricot jam. Use the pastry trimmings to make Palmiers (page 27).

Roll out the pastry to a 30 × 36 cm/12 × 14 inch rectangle. Trim the edges of the pastry and cut in half down the shorter length. Place 1 piece on a dampened baking sheet and brush the edge with egg or water. Sift a little flour over the surface of the other piece of pastry and fold in half lengthwise. (The flour will prevent the pastry sticking together.) With a small knife cut out the centre, leaving a 2.5 cm/1 inch border. Open out the pastry, brush off the surplus flour and carefully lift on to the larger piece of pastry. Make certain the edges are neat all the way round and press down well. Knock up the edge of the pastry.
Mark the top of the border in a lattice pattern and prick the base of the tart well. Leave to rest for 20 minutes in the refrigerator. Place in a preheated oven and bake for 20 minutes or until golden brown and cooked through. Cool on a wire tray.
When the pastry is cold, brush the base with hot sieved apricot jam and allow to cool. Pipe or spoon the cream in an even layer in the bottom of the tart. Cut the strawberries into halves or quarters, according to size, and arrange in diagonal lines on top of the cream. Boil the jam and jelly separately, if necessary whisk the redcurrant jelly until smooth. Brush the top and sides of the pastry with hot apricot jam and glaze the fruit well with the hot redcurrant jelly. Allow to cool. Eat on the same day.
Serves 6

Choux aux fraises

Metric	Imperial
65 g Choux Pastry (page 10)	2½ oz Choux Pastry (page 10)
Sauce:	**Sauce:**
150 ml milk	¼ pint milk
2 egg yolks	2 egg yolks
40 g caster sugar	1½ oz caster sugar
1 × 2.5 ml spoon vanilla essence	½ teaspoon vanilla essence
225 g strawberries, hulled and sieved	8 oz strawberries, hulled and sieved
150 ml double or whipping cream, whipped	¼ pint double or whipping cream, whipped
To finish:	**To finish:**
4 × 15 ml spoons double or whipping cream, whipped	4 tablespoons double or whipping cream, whipped
225 g strawberries, hulled	8 oz strawberries, hulled
2 × 5 ml spoons caster sugar	2 teaspoons caster sugar

Preparation time: 1 hour, plus chilling
Cooking time: 40 minutes
Oven: 220°C, 425°F, Gas Mark 7;
        190°C, 375°F, Gas Mark 5

Place the choux pastry in a piping bag fitted with a 1 cm/½ inch plain nozzle. Pipe 8 large oval shapes on a greased baking sheet. Place in a preheated oven and bake for 15 minutes. Reduce the oven temperature and continue cooking for a further 25 minutes until crisp and golden brown. Cut the choux ovals across in half before placing on a wire tray to cool.
For the sauce, warm the milk in a saucepan. Cream the egg yolks, sugar and vanilla essence together. Pour the warm milk on to the mixture and stir together. Return to the pan and stir continuously until it thickens sufficiently to coat the back of a wooden spoon. Remove from the heat and strain into a bowl. When cool, stir in the sieved strawberries and cream. Chill well.
To finish, fill the choux ovals with the whipped cream and top with 175 g/6 oz of the strawberries which can be left whole or sliced. Replace the tops and pile them in a serving dish. Just before serving, pour over the chilled sauce. Garnish with the rest of the strawberries.
Eat on the same day.
Makes 8

From the top: Choux aux fraises; Tranche aux fruits

TEATIME PASTRIES

Sunday teatime with tables groaning with a fine selection of cakes and pastries was one of our English traditions, and there is still always the occasion when small mouth-watering pastries can be served. Whether you choose a regional speciality such as Coventry Godcakes or Eccles Cakes, or rich Eclairs and fruity Canelle Tartelettes, this chapter will provide the answer.

Coconut slices

Metric	Imperial
225 g Shortcrust Pastry (page 6), chilled	8 oz Shortcrust Pastry (page 6), chilled
4 × 15 ml spoons jam	4 tablespoons jam

Topping:	Topping:
2 egg whites	2 egg whites
100 g caster sugar	4 oz caster sugar
1 × 15 ml spoon plain flour	1 tablespoon plain flour
100 g desiccated coconut	4 oz desiccated coconut

Preparation time: 20 minutes
Cooking time: 30 minutes
Oven: 180°C, 350°F, Gas Mark 4

Roll out the pastry and use to line an 18 × 28 cm/7 × 11 inch shallow tin. Spread the jam in a layer over the pastry.
Whisk the egg whites until stiff and standing in peaks. Fold in the sugar, flour and coconut, and spread over the pastry. Place in a preheated oven and bake for 30 minutes. Cool for 5 minutes before cutting into slices and removing from the tin. Cool on a wire tray.
Keeps up to 7 days in an airtight tin.
Makes 12 slices

From the left: Pineapple tartlets; Coconut slices; Palmiers

Palmiers

Metric
225 g Puff Pastry (page 9), see method
40 g caster sugar

Imperial
8 oz Puff Pastry (page 9), see method
1½ oz caster sugar

Preparation time: 15 minutes, plus chilling
Cooking time: 20–25 minutes
Oven: 220°C, 425°F, Gas Mark 7

Make up the puff pastry, giving it only 4 rolls and folds instead of 6, and chill. Continue rolling and folding twice using the sugar instead of flour to roll it. Chill the pastry for about 20 minutes.

Roll out to a 36 × 30 cm/14 × 12 inch rectangle. Trim the edges and fold the long sides to the centre, then bring the folded edge to the centre on each side so that you have a long strip of folded pastry about 6 cm/2½ inches wide. Press together using the side of the hand. Trim the ends then slice into 1 cm/½ inch pieces. Place them on dampened baking sheets with the cut side upwards. They must be well spaced out as they spread sideways. Chill for 10 minutes.

Place in a preheated oven and bake for 10 minutes, turn over with a palette or round ended knife and bake until caramelized to a toffee brown, which takes a further 10–15 minutes. Cool on a wire tray.

Keeps up to 7 days in an airtight tin.
Makes 24

Pineapple tartlets

Metric
100 g plain flour
25 g caster sugar
50 g butter
25 g flaked almonds, lightly chopped
1 egg yolk
3 × 5 ml spoons water

Imperial
4 oz plain flour
1 oz caster sugar
2 oz butter
1 oz flaked almonds, lightly chopped
1 egg yolk
3 teaspoons water

To decorate:
225 ml double or whipping cream, whipped
1 × 225 g can pineapple slices, drained and chopped
glacé cherries
crystallized angelica

To decorate:
7½ fl oz double or whipping cream, whipped
1 × 8 oz can pineapple slices, drained and chopped
glacé cherries
crystallized angelica

Preparation time: 25 minutes
Cooking time: 12–15 minutes
Oven: 190°C, 375°F, Gas Mark 5

These tartlets are suitable for a buffet. If fresh pineapple is available, this can be peeled, sliced, cored and cut into segments.

Sift the flour and sugar into a bowl. Rub in the butter until the mixture resembles fine breadcrumbs. Add the chopped almonds and bind together with the egg yolk and water. Knead lightly, then roll out thinly and cut into 7.5 cm/3 inch circles. Place in greased tartlet tins and prick the pastry well. Place in a preheated oven and bake for 12–15 minutes until lightly coloured. Remove from the tins and cool on a wire tray. Spoon the cream into a piping bag fitted with a large rosette nozzle and pipe a large swirl into each pastry case. Place 4 pieces of chopped pineapple on the top of each tartlet, decorate with a small piece of glacé cherry and angelica leaves in the centre.

Empty cases keep up to 4 days in an airtight tin. When filled, eat on the same day.
Makes 14–16

Eccles cakes

Preparation time: 25 minutes
Cooking time: 15 minutes
Oven: 220°C, 425°F, Gas Mark 7

Metric	Imperial
100 g Flaky Pastry (page 8), chilled	4 oz Flaky Pastry (page 8), chilled

Filling:

25 g butter	1 oz butter
100 g currants	4 oz currants
25 g candied peel, chopped	1 oz candied peel, chopped
25 g sugar	1 oz sugar
1 × 2.5 ml spoon mixed spice	½ teaspoon mixed spice
1 × 1.25 ml spoon nutmeg	¼ teaspoon nutmeg

To finish:

1 egg white, lightly whisked	1 egg white, lightly whisked
little caster sugar	little caster sugar

For the filling, melt the butter in a pan and remove from the heat. Stir in the remaining filling ingredients.

Roll out the pastry and cut into eight 14 cm/5½ inch circles – a saucer makes a useful guide. Put a spoonful of filling on each circle of pastry and dampen the edge with a little water. Fold the pastry into the centre, turn it over and shape into a round. Press flat using gentle pressure with a rolling pin to flatten each one. Brush with the egg white and sprinkle with a little sugar. Place on a baking sheet and make 3–4 slashes across the top of each with a sharp knife. Place in a preheated oven and bake for 15 minutes. Cool on a wire tray.

Keeps up to 7 days in a airtight tin.

Makes 8

Coventry godcakes

Preparation time: 15 minutes, plus chilling
Cooking time: 25 minutes
Oven: 220°C, 425°F, Gas Mark 7

Metric	Imperial
225 g Flaky Pastry (page 8), chilled	8 oz Flaky Pastry (page 8), chilled
100 g mincemeat	4 oz mincemeat
1 egg white, lightly whisked	1 egg white, lightly whisked
little caster sugar	little caster sugar

Roll out the pastry to a 20 × 41 cm/8 × 16 inch rectangle. Cut in half lengthways and then each piece into eight 10 cm/4 inch triangles.

Place a spoonful of mincemeat on half of them and dampen the edges of the pastry. Put the second piece on top and seal. Place on a baking sheet and chill for 10 minutes. Place in a preheated oven and bake for 20 minutes. Brush with the egg white, sprinkle with caster sugar and return to the oven for 5 minutes.

Keeps up to 7 days in an airtight tin.

Makes 8

Apple and date slices

Preparation time: 20 minutes
Cooking time: 40 minutes
Oven: 200°C, 400°F, Gas Mark 6

Metric	Imperial
225 g Wholemeal Shortcrust Pastry (page 6)	8 oz Wholemeal Shortcrust Pastry (page 6)
350 g cooking apples, peeled, cored and roughly chopped	12 oz cooking apples, peeled, cored and roughly chopped
100 g dates, chopped	4 oz dates, chopped
50 g walnuts, chopped	2 oz walnuts, chopped
50 g brown sugar	2 oz brown sugar

Topping:

225 g wholemeal flour	8 oz wholemeal flour
100 g butter or margarine	4 oz butter or margarine
25 g soft brown sugar	1 oz soft brown sugar
1 × 2.5 ml spoon ground cinnamon	½ teaspoon ground cinnamon

Roll out the pastry and use to line a greased 18 × 28 cm/7 × 11 inch shallow tin. Trim the edges. Place the apples, dates, walnuts and brown sugar into a bowl and stir together. Spread in a layer over the pastry.

For the topping, put the flour into a bowl and rub in the butter or margarine. When finely mixed, blend in the sugar and cinnamon. Sprinkle in a layer to cover the topping. Place in a preheated oven and bake for 40 minutes. Remove from the oven and cut into 12–16 slices. Allow to cool, then remove from the tin and place on a wire tray until cold.

Keeps in an airtight tin up to 2 days.

Makes 12–16

From the top, clockwise: Eccles cakes; Coventry godcakes; Apple and date slices

Chocolate éclairs

Metric
65 g Choux Pastry (page 10)
250 ml double or whipping cream, lightly whipped

Imperial
2½ oz Choux Pastry (page 10)
8 fl oz double or whipping cream, lightly whipped

Chocolate icing:
50 g plain chocolate, cut into small pieces
100 g icing sugar, sifted
1 × 15 ml spoon hot water
1 × 5 ml spoon oil

Chocolate icing:
2 oz plain chocolate, cut into small pieces
4 oz icing sugar, sifted
1 tablespoon hot water
1 teaspoon oil

Preparation time: 30 minutes, plus cooling
Cooking time: 30–40 minutes
Oven: 220°C, 425°F, Gas Mark 7;
　　　190°C, 375°F, Gas Mark 5

Chocolate Eclairs are a great favourite at all times. Small ones about 4 cm/1½ inches long are ideal for Petits Fours. For teatime, pipe them into 6 cm/2½ inch lengths about the size of a little finger. Eclairs can be frozen very satisfactorily. Make, fill and ice them and place in a single layer in polythene boxes or foil trays. Freeze uncovered then cover with the lids, or place the foil trays in polythene bags and seal well. Remove the lid or covering before thawing for 1½–2 hours at room temperature.

Place the pastry in a piping bag fitted with a 1 cm/½ inch plain nozzle and pipe into lengths on a lightly greased baking sheet. Put one tray at a time into a preheated oven and bake for 10 minutes, then reduce the oven temperature and bake for a further 20–30 minutes until the éclairs are crisp and golden brown. Remove from the oven and pierce a hole at one end of each. If necessary, return to the oven for a few more minutes to dry out. Cool on a wire tray.

Meanwhile, make the chocolate icing. Melt the chocolate pieces in a bowl over a small pan of hot water. Add the sifted icing sugar, water and oil and stir until smooth. If necessary add a little more water to give a coating consistency. Remove from the heat and cool slightly.

When the éclairs are cold, spoon the cream into a piping bag fitted with a 5 mm/¼ inch plain nozzle and fill the éclairs through the hole at the end. Dip the top of each éclair into the chocolate icing and allow just a little icing to run over the hole to cover it. Keep in a cool place until served.

Eat on the same day.

Makes 12–16 6 cm/2½ inch éclairs

Danish cream tarts

Metric	Imperial
15 g plain flour	½ oz plain flour
25 g caster sugar	1 oz caster sugar
1 egg yolk	1 egg yolk
250 ml single cream	8 fl oz single cream
150 g Pâte Sucrée (page 8)	5 oz Pâte Sucrée (page 8)
175–225 g fresh or frozen black cherries, stoned and quartered	6–8 oz fresh or frozen black cherries, stoned and quartered
little icing sugar, to finish	little icing sugar, to finish

Preparation time: 30 minutes
Cooking time: about 25–30 minutes
Oven: 200°C, 375°F, Gas Mark 5

Blend the flour, sugar and egg yolk together until smooth. Heat the cream, just before it boils pour on to the mixture and blend well. Return to the heat and, stirring continuously, bring to the boil and cook for 2–3 minutes. Allow to cool, giving the cream an occasional beat to prevent a skin forming.
Roll out the pastry thinly and cut an equal number of 7.5 cm/3 inch and 6 cm/2½ inch circles. Place the larger circles in greased deep bun tins. When the cream is cold, put a layer in the bottom of each tart. Place quartered cherries on top. Dampen the edges of the remaining circles, cover each tart and seal well. Place in a preheated oven and bake for 25–30 minutes. Remove from the bun tins and cool on a wire tray. Sift an even layer of icing sugar over the tops of the tarts and serve cold.
Eat on the same day.
Makes 10–12

Cream horns

Metric	Imperial
225 g Flaky Pastry (page 8), chilled	8 oz Flaky Pastry (page 8), chilled
lightly whisked egg white, or water	lightly whisked egg white, or water
1 × 15 ml spoon caster sugar	1 tablespoon caster sugar
2 × 15 ml spoons raspberry jam	2 tablespoons raspberry jam
250 ml double or whipping cream, whipped	8 fl oz double or whipping cream, whipped

Preparation time: 30 minutes
Cooking time: 15–20 minutes
Oven: 220°C, 425°F, Gas Mark 7

Cream Horns are also an excellent way of using puff pastry trimmings. Place the trimmings neatly on top of each other, roll out to a rectangle and fold in three, the same way as folding flaky or puff pastry. Rest the pastry in the refrigerator before using.

Roll out the pastry thinly to a 45 × 30 cm/18 × 12 inch rectangle. Trim the edges and cut lengthways into 10 strips. Cut a small piece diagonally from one end of each strip to make a point. Brush the strips with water. Place the point of the horn tin against the point of the pastry. Wind the strip around the tin so that it overlaps about 1 cm/½ inch at each turn. Place on a dampened baking sheet and put in the refrigerator for 20 minutes to rest. Brush with lightly beaten egg white or water and sprinkle with the sugar. Place in a preheated oven and bake for 15–20 minutes until golden brown. Remove the horns from the tins with a slight twisting action. Cool on a wire rack.
Heat the jam until it has melted and, with a teaspoon, pour a little into the point of each horn. When the pastry and the jam are completely cold, spoon the cream into a piping bag fitted with a large rosette nozzle and fill each horn with a large swirl of cream. Keep cool until served.
Empty cases keep up to 7 days in an airtight tin. When filled, eat on the same day.
Makes 10

From the top: Cream horns; Danish cream tarts; Chocolate éclairs

Chestnut boats

Preparation time: 25 minutes
Cooking time: 10–12 minutes
Oven: 190°C, 375°F, Gas Mark 5

Metric
65 g Pâte Sucrée (page 8)
225 g unsweetened chestnut purée
25–50 g caster sugar
3 × 15 ml spoons brandy
6 × 15 ml spoons double or whipping cream, stiffly whipped

Imperial
2½ oz Pâte Sucrée (page 8)
8 oz unsweetened chestnut purée
1–2 oz caster sugar
3 tablespoons brandy
6 tablespoons double or whipping cream, stiffly whipped

To decorate:
glacé cherries
crystallized angelica

To decorate:
glacé cherries
crystallized angelica

These tartlets are quick and easy to make. If you like the chestnut purée to be sweeter, then add more sugar to your taste. You can also add a little more brandy if you prefer a stronger flavour.

Roll out the pastry thinly and use to line 9.5 cm/3¾ inch boat-shaped tartlet tins. Prick the pastry well, place in a preheated oven and bake for 10–12 minutes. Remove carefully from the tins and cool on a wire tray.
Blend the chestnut purée, caster sugar and brandy together in a bowl until the sugar has dissolved. Fold the cream into the mixture. Spoon the chestnut cream into a piping bag fitted with a large star nozzle and pipe a wavy line down the centre of each pastry boat. Decorate the centre of each boat with a small piece of glacé cherry and 2 angelica leaves.
Empty cases keep up to 4 days in an airtight tin. When filled, eat on the same day.
Makes 18–20

From the top left, clockwise: Canelle tartelettes;
Chocolate and rum tartlets; Chestnut boats

Chocolate and rum tartlets

Metric	Imperial
65 g Pâte Sucrée (page 8)	2½ oz Pâte Sucrée (page 8)
2 × 15 ml spoons rum	2 tablespoons rum
2 × 15 ml spoons grated plain chocolate	2 tablespoons grated plain chocolate
120 ml double or whipping cream, whipped	4 fl oz double or whipping cream, whipped

Icing:

Metric	Imperial
100 g icing sugar, sifted	4 oz icing sugar, sifted
1 × 15 ml spoon water	1 tablespoon water
1 × 15 ml spoon rum	1 tablespoon rum
green food colouring	green food colouring

Preparation time: 20 minutes, plus resting
Cooking time: 12–15 minutes
Oven: 190°C, 375°F, Gas Mark 5

These tartlets are easy to make. If the pastry cases are made in advance, they can be kept in an airtight tin and quickly filled when required.

Roll out the pastry thinly and cut into 7.5 cm/3 inch circles using a fluted cutter. Place in tartlet tins and prick the bases well. Put in the refrigerator for 20 minutes to rest. Place in a preheated oven and bake for 10–12 minutes until golden brown. Remove from the tins and cool on a wire tray.
Stir the rum and grated chocolate into the cream. Fill each tartlet case three-quarters full and smooth the top carefully, making sure that the cream does not mark the edge of the tartlet.
Mix the icing sugar with the water and rum. Add 1–2 drops of green food colouring to make a pale green icing and, using a teaspoon, pour a little over the cream so that the top of the tartlet is completely coated. Leave in a cool place until served.
Keeps up to 2 days.
Makes about 10

Variations:
Use Crème de Menthe or a little peppermint essence instead of rum.
Orange blends well with chocolate, so use an orange-flavoured liqueur with the cream and orange juice with orange food colouring to make the icing.

Canelle tartelettes

Metric	Imperial
100 g plain flour	4 oz plain flour
50 g caster sugar	2 oz caster sugar
1½ × 5 ml spoons ground cinnamon	1½ teaspoons ground cinnamon
50 g butter	2 oz butter
2 egg yolks	2 egg yolks

Filling:

Metric	Imperial
350 g blackcurrants	12 oz blackcurrants
150 ml water	¼ pint water
75 g sugar	3 oz sugar
3 × 5 ml spoons arrowroot	3 teaspoons arrowroot
225 ml double or whipping cream, whipped, to decorate	7½ fl oz double or whipping cream, whipped, to decorate

Preparation time: 30 minutes, plus chilling
Cooking time: 15 minutes
Oven: 190°C, 375°F, Gas Mark 5

These tartlets will prove a great favourite for the tea table and are also ideal to serve at a buffet. Fresh or frozen blackcurrants are the best choice. Canned blackcurrants can be used, 2 × 425 g/15 oz cans will be needed, with no sugar. As canned blackcurrants are already cooked, just drain the blackcurrants and thicken 150 ml/¼ pint of the juice with the arrowroot.

Sift the flour, sugar and cinnamon on to a board or into a bowl. Make a well in the centre, add the butter and the egg yolks and blend with the flour. Knead lightly until a smooth dough is formed. Wrap the pastry in greaseproof paper or cling film and chill in the refrigerator for 20 minutes. Roll out the pastry thinly and cut into 7.5 cm/3 inch circles. Place in greased tartlet tins and prick the pastry well. Place in a preheated oven and bake for about 15 minutes. Remove from the tins and cool on a wire tray.
Meanwhile, remove the stalks from fresh blackcurrants and wash well. Frozen blackcurrants need not be thawed. Place in a saucepan with the water and sugar and simmer gently for about 15 minutes until tender. Remove the blackcurrants from the syrup with a slotted spoon and boil the syrup to reduce it slightly. Slake the arrowroot in a little water, add to the syrup and boil again, stirring all the time until it becomes very thick. Return the blackcurrants to the mixture and allow to cool. Spoon into the cold tartlet cases. When the filling is cold, spoon the cream into a piping bag fitted with a large rosette nozzle and pipe a large swirl of cream on the top of each tartlet.
Empty cases keep up to 4 days in an airtight tin. When filled, eat on the same day.
Makes 14–16

Almond dartois

Metric	Imperial
50 g butter	2 oz butter
50 g caster sugar	2 oz caster sugar
1 egg, lightly beaten	1 egg, lightly beaten
50 g ground almonds	2 oz ground almonds
1 × 15 ml spoon rum or lemon juice	1 tablespoon rum or lemon juice
100 g Puff Pastry (page 9), chilled	4 oz Puff Pastry (page 9), chilled
1 egg, beaten with a pinch of salt	1 egg, beaten with a pinch of salt
little icing sugar	little icing sugar

Preparation time: 20 minutes, plus chilling
Cooking time: 30 minutes
Oven: 220°C, 425°F, Gas Mark 7;
      200°C, 400°F, Gas Mark 6

These are crisp, flaky fingers of puff pastry with an almond filling. They are baked in a strip and then cut into fingers afterwards. The sugar glaze should be a rich toffee brown, and special care is needed to make sure this does not burn.

Cream the butter and sugar together until light and fluffy. Beat in the egg, a little at a time, and then stir in the ground almonds and rum or lemon juice.
Cut the pastry in half, and roll out one piece at a time to a 25 cm/10 inch square. Trim the edges and cut in half. Place on a dampened baking sheet. Brush the edge with beaten egg and spread half the almond filling on the pastry, leaving a 1 cm/½ inch border round the edge.
Place the second piece of pastry on top and seal the edges by pressing firmly with the side of your hand. Mark firmly into 5 without cutting through the dough. Repeat with the rest of the pastry. Chill for 10 minutes.
Brush the pastry with beaten egg and mark a line down the centre of each, then mark lines at an angle to this to form a chevron pattern. Do this with the back of a small vegetable knife held like a pen.
Place in a preheated oven and bake for 10 minutes. Quickly sift the icing sugar over the top, reduce the oven temperature and continue to bake for a further 15–20 minutes until the sugar has melted and caramelized. Reduce the oven temperature again if the glaze becomes too dark. Cool on a wire tray. Cut into fingers to serve.
Keeps up to 7 days in an airtight tin.
Makes 10

Conversations

Metric	Imperial
100 g Flaky Pastry (page 8), chilled	4 oz Flaky Pastry (page 8), chilled

Filling:

Metric	Imperial
50 g butter	2 oz butter
50 g caster sugar	2 oz caster sugar
1 egg, beaten	1 egg, beaten
50 g ground almonds	2 oz ground almonds
1 × 15 ml spoon lemon juice	1 tablespoon lemon juice

To finish:

Metric	Imperial
1 egg white	1 egg white
225 g icing sugar, sifted	8 oz icing sugar, sifted
1 × 5 ml spoon plain flour	1 teaspoon plain flour

Preparation time: 15 minutes
Cooking time: 17–20 minutes
Oven: 190°C, 375°F, Gas Mark 5

These iced tartlets have a moist almond filling in crisp pastry cases and an unusual baked icing.

Cream the butter and sugar together until light and fluffy. Beat in the egg, a little at a time, and then stir in the ground almonds and lemon juice.
Put the egg white into a bowl, add half the icing sugar and stir well. Blend in the flour, then stir in enough of the remaining icing sugar to give a thick consistency. Roll out the pastry thinly and cut into eighteen 7.5 cm/3 inch circles using a fluted cutter. Place in bun tins and prick the pastry well. Fold the pastry trimmings together, keeping them in layers. Roll once into a rectangle, fold and chill, ready to use later.
Divide the almond cream filling between the pastry cases and put a spoonful of the icing on each one. Roll the pastry trimmings thinly and cut into 5 mm/¼ inch strips. Cut into short lengths to fit across the tartlets and put 2 strips side by side on each one. Place in a preheated oven and bake for 17–20 minutes until the pastry is cooked and the icing baked to a shiny fawn layer. Watch them carefully towards the end of baking as they will burn quickly if cooked too long.
Keeps up to 3 days in an airtight tin.
Makes 18

Sacristans

Metric
100 g Puff Pastry (page 9), chilled
1 egg, beaten
40 g flaked almonds
2 × 5 ml spoons caster sugar

Imperial
4 oz Puff Pastry (page 9), chilled
1 egg, beaten
1½ oz flaked almonds
2 teaspoons caster sugar

Preparation time: 15 minutes
Cooking time: 8–10 minutes
Oven: 220°C, 425°F, Gas Mark 7

Roll out the pastry to a 30 × 45 cm/12 × 18 inch rectangle. Cut across in half lengthways to give two 15 cm/6 inch strips. Trim the edges and brush all over the surface of each piece with the beaten egg. Sprinkle with the flaked almonds, pressing these on firmly and then sprinkle with the sugar. Cut into 1 cm/½ inch wide strips.

Twist each strip as it is put on dampened baking sheet and press the ends down firmly to hold them in shape. Place in a preheated oven and bake for 8–10 minutes until golden brown, well risen and crisp. Watch them carefully for the last 2–3 minutes as they will burn quickly if cooked too long.

Keeps up to 7 days in an airtight tin.

Makes 36

From the back left, clockwise: Sacristans; Conversations; Almond dartois

PASTRY SAVOURIES

Instead of the usual dish of potato crisps or peanuts, serve some pastry savouries to your guests. A plate of cheese straws or assorted canapés is a welcome addition when drinks are being served. If there is a meal to follow choose small, light pastries, such as the Nutty Cheese Bites.

On other occasions, serve a larger selection, you might have some cheese dips and vegetables to dunk in them, as a colourful contrast. Cheese and wine parties can be made more exciting with some homemade cheesy pastries.

Time can be a problem in preparing these, so it is often best to make the pastries, such as cheese biscuits, and store in an airtight container or in the freezer. They are then ready to decorate on the day they are to be eaten.

As pastry savouries must not be too large, a set of small fancy cutters can be useful, though triangles, squares and rectangles can all be cut with only a sharp knife to aid you. If you are only making a small number of canapés, toppings can be spread on with a knife; but if there are a number to do it is much faster, as well as more attractive, to put on the fillings using a piping bag and nozzle.

Barquettes aux crevettes; Bouchées

Bouchées

Metric	Imperial
100 g Puff Pastry (page 9), chilled	4 oz Puff Pastry (page 9), chilled
1 egg, beaten	1 egg, beaten

Filling:

Metric	Imperial
65 g butter	$2\frac{1}{2}$ oz butter
50 g mushrooms, chopped	2 oz mushrooms, chopped
15 g plain flour	$\frac{1}{2}$ oz plain flour
150 ml chicken stock	$\frac{1}{4}$ pint chicken stock
1 chicken joint, cooked and finely chopped	1 chicken joint, cooked and finely chopped
dash of Tabasco	dash of Tabasco
salt	salt
freshly ground white pepper	freshly ground white pepper

Preparation time: 30 minutes
Cooking time: 10–15 minutes
Oven: 220°C, 425°F, Gas Mark 7

Roll out the pastry 5 mm/$\frac{1}{4}$ inch thick. Cut into circles, using a 4 cm/$1\frac{1}{2}$ inch cutter. Put on a baking sheet. Brush with beaten egg and mark the centre with a smaller cutter. Place in a preheated oven and bake for 10–15 minutes until well risen, crisp and golden.
For the filling, melt 50 g/2 oz of the butter, add the mushrooms and cook over a medium heat for about 3 minutes. Put aside.
Melt the remaining butter, add the flour and cook for a few minutes, stirring. Remove from the heat and add the stock slowly, stirring continuously. Bring to the boil and simmer for 4–5 minutes. Stir in the mushrooms, finely chopped chicken, Tabasco and salt and pepper to taste.
When the pastry cases are cooked, cool them on a wire tray. Lift off the lids and scrape out any undercooked pastry. Fill with the chicken mixture and replace the lids. Serve hot or cold.
Empty cases keep up to 10 days in an airtight tin. Reheat before using.
Makes 30

Barquettes aux crevettes

Metric	Imperial
50 g Cheese Pastry (page 7)	2 oz Cheese Pastry (page 7)
25 g butter	1 oz butter
25 g plain flour	1 oz plain flour
250 ml milk	8 fl oz milk
1 × 2.5 ml spoon tomato purée	$\frac{1}{2}$ teaspoon tomato purée
salt	salt
freshly ground white pepper	freshly ground white pepper
100 g shelled prawns	4 oz shelled prawns
small sprigs of parsley, to garnish	small sprigs of parsley, to garnish

Preparation time: 30–40 minutes, plus chilling
Cooking time: 12–15 minutes
Oven: 200°C, 400°F, Gas Mark 6

Roll out the pastry thinly and use to line twenty four 7.5 cm/3 inch boat shaped tartlet tins. Prick the bases well and put on a baking sheet. Place in a preheated oven and bake for 12–15 minutes until light golden brown. Remove from the tins and cool on a wire tray. Melt the butter in a small saucepan over a gentle heat. Add the flour and cook for 2–3 minutes, stirring. Remove from the heat and add the milk, a little at a time. Return to the heat, bring to the boil, stirring continuously, and cook for a further 2–3 minutes. Add the tomato purée, salt and pepper to taste.
Reserve 12 small whole prawns and chop the remainder. Add to the sauce and mix well. Fill each barquette with the mixture and top each with half a prawn and a small sprig of parsley.
Empty cases keep up to 10 days in an airtight tin. When filled, eat on the same day.
Makes 24

Variations:
Soften 100 g/4 oz full fat soft cheese with a little single cream. Place in a piping bag filled with a small star nozzle and fill each barquette. Garnish with a little lumpfish roe.
Sieve 100 g/4 oz smooth pâté and mix with 2 × 5 ml spoons/2 teaspoons sherry. Pipe into the pastry boats and garnish with a slice of gherkin.

From the left: Cheese straws; York fingers; Cheese palmiers; Nutty cheese bites

Cheese straws

Metric
*100 g Cheese Pastry
(page 7)*

Imperial
*4 oz Cheese Pastry
(page 7)*

Preparation time: 15 minutes
Cooking time: 10–15 minutes
Oven: 200°C, 400°F, Gas Mark 6

Roll out the pastry to about 5 mm/¼ inch thick. Cut
out 6 rings using a 5 cm/2 inch plain cutter and cut out
the centres with a 4 cm/1½ inch plain cutter. Cut the
rest of the pastry into straws about 6 cm/2½ inch long
by 5 mm/¼ inch wide.
Gather the trimmings together and roll out again and
cut out more straws with all the remaining pastry.
Arrange on a greased baking sheet. Place in a preheated oven and bake for 10–15 minutes until golden
brown. Cool on a wire tray.
Place some of the cheese straws through the centres of
the rings and arrange around the edge of a plate. Put
the rest of the straws in the centre of the plate.
Keeps up to 10 days in an airtight tin.
Makes 60

Variation:
Dip the ends of each straw into a mild paprika to give
red tips.

York fingers

Metric
*175 g lean streaky bacon,
rind removed, diced
100 g Flaky Pastry
(page 8), chilled
2 × 5 ml spoons French
mustard
little beaten egg
50 g cheese, grated*

Imperial
*6 oz lean streaky bacon,
rind removed, diced
4 oz Flaky Pastry (page
8), chilled
2 teaspoons French
mustard
little beaten egg
2 oz cheese, grated*

Preparation time: 20 minutes
Cooking time: 15 minutes
Oven: 220°C, 425°F, Gas Mark 7

Fry the bacon until crisp, using no extra fat. Drain on
paper towels.
Roll out the pastry thinly to a 30 cm/12 inch square.
Cut in half and spread one piece of the pastry with
mustard. Cover with the bacon and place the second
piece of pastry on top. Brush with beaten egg and
sprinkle with the grated cheese.
Cut into 7.5 × 2.5 cm/3 × 1 inch fingers and put on a
baking sheet. Place in a preheated oven and bake for
15 minutes or until golden brown and cooked
through. Serve hot or cold.
Keeps up to 2 days in an airtight tin in the
refrigerator.
Makes 24

Cheese palmiers

Metric	*Imperial*
100 g Puff Pastry (page 9), see method	*4 oz Puff Pastry (page 9), see method*
2 × 15 ml spoons grated Parmesan cheese	*2 tablespoons grated Parmesan cheese*

Preparation time: 20 minutes, plus chilling
Cooking time: 20 minutes
Oven: 220°C, 425°F, Gas Mark 7

Make the puff pastry giving it 4 rolls and folds only.
Chill thoroughly. Roll and fold twice more, sprink-
ling the cheese on to the pastry at the same time.
Roll out to a 36 × 30 cm/14 × 12 inch rectangle. Trim
the edges and fold the long sides to the centre. Bring
the folded edge to the centre on each side, making a
long strip of folded pastry about 6 cm/2½ inches wide.
Press together using the side of the hand. Trim the
ends, then slice into 1 cm/½ inch pieces. Put these on
dampened baking sheets with the cut side upwards.
They must be well spaced out as they spread sideways.
Chill for 10 minutes.
Place in a preheated oven and bake for 10 minutes.
Turn them over with a palette or round ended knife
and bake for a further 10 minutes or until both sides
are golden brown. Cool on a wire tray.
Keeps up to 5 days in an airtight tin.
Makes 25

Nutty cheese bites

Metric	*Imperial*
50 g Cheese Pastry (page 7)	*2 oz Cheese Pastry (page 7)*
1 egg, beaten	*1 egg, beaten*
blanched almonds, walnuts or hazelnuts	*blanched almonds, walnuts or hazelnuts*

Preparation time: 15 minutes
Cooking time: 12–15 minutes
Oven: 200°C, 400°F, Gas Mark 6

Roll out the pastry 5 mm/¼ inch thick and cut into 2.5
cm/1 inch rounds, squares and diamonds.
Place on a greased baking sheet and brush with beaten
egg. Place a nut on each savoury biscuit. Place in a
preheated oven and bake for 10–15 minutes until
golden brown. Cool on a wire tray.
Keeps up to 10 days in an airtight tin.
Makes 24

Sardine crescents

Metric

Pastry:
100 g plain flour, sifted
1 × 1.25 ml spoon salt
50 g butter, cut in pieces
100 g cottage cheese,
   sieved

Filling:
2 plump canned sardines
freshly ground black
   pepper
pinch of cayenne
1 × 5 ml spoon finely
   chopped fresh parsley
1 egg, beaten

Imperial

Pastry:
4 oz plain flour, sifted
¼ teaspoon salt
2 oz butter, cut in pieces
4 oz cottage cheese,
   sieved

Filling:
2 plump canned sardines
freshly ground black
   pepper
pinch of cayenne
1 teaspoon finely chopped
   fresh parsley
1 egg, beaten

Preparation time: 30 minutes, plus chilling
Cooking time: 15 minutes
Oven: 200°C, 400°F, Gas Mark 6

Place the flour and salt into a bowl and rub in the butter, using the fingertips, until the mixture resembles fine breadcrumbs. Stir in the cottage cheese. Bind together to make a smooth ball of dough. Wrap and chill for 30 minutes.
Mash the sardines, season with black pepper and cayenne. Stir in the parsley.
Roll out the chilled pastry thinly to a square and cut into six 10 cm/4 inch squares. Divide each one diagonally in half to give 2 triangles. Put a little of the sardine mixture on each one and roll up into a crescent shape like croissants. Dampen the top of the pastry with egg and press down firmly.
Put on a baking sheet and brush again with beaten egg. Place in a preheated oven and bake for 15 minutes. Cool on a wire tray.
Keeps for 1 day.
Makes 12

Petits choux

Metric
65 g Choux Pastry (page
   10)
1 egg, beaten
1 × 200 g can salmon
1 × 5 ml spoon lemon
   juice (optional)
2 × 15 ml spoons soured
   cream or mayonnaise
salt
freshly ground black
   pepper
little red pimento or red
   pepper, to garnish

Imperial
2½ oz Choux Pastry
   (page 10)
1 egg, beaten
1 × 7 oz can salmon
1 teaspoon lemon
   juice (optional)
2 tablespoons soured
   cream or mayonnaise
salt
freshly ground black
   pepper
little red pimento or red
   pepper, to garnish

Preparation time: 20 minutes
Cooking time: 25–35 minutes
Oven: 220°C, 425°F, Gas Mark 7;
       190°C, 375°F, Gas Mark 5

Put the choux pastry into a piping bag fitted with a 1 cm/½ inch plain nozzle. Pipe small balls on to a lightly greased baking sheet. Brush with beaten egg.
Place in a preheated oven and bake for 10 minutes, then reduce the oven temperature and bake for a further 15–25 minutes until the balls are crisp and a light golden brown. Make a diagonal cut halfway down each choux ball, sloping to the back and taking care not to cut the ball completely through. Cool on a wire tray.
Remove the bones from the salmon and mash it in a bowl. Mix in the lemon juice (if using), soured cream or mayonnaise, salt and pepper. Fill the balls with the mashed salmon filling. Place a small square of pimento or red pepper on the front of the filling.
Unfilled pastry keeps for 1 day in an airtight tin. When filled, eat on the same day.
Makes 60

Talmouse of smoked haddock

Metric	Imperial
15 g butter	*½ oz butter*
15 g plain flour	*½ oz plain flour*
150 ml milk	*¼ pint milk*
75 g smoked haddock, cooked	*3 oz smoked haddock, cooked*
25 g butter	*1 oz butter*
40 g cheese, grated	*1½ oz cheese, grated*
salt	*salt*
freshly ground black pepper	*freshly ground black pepper*
225 g Cheese Pastry (page 7)	*8 oz Cheese Pastry (page 7)*

Petits choux; Sardine crescents; Talmouse of smoked haddock

Preparation time: 25 minutes
Cooking time: 12–15 minutes
Oven: 200°C, 400°F, Gas Mark 6

Melt the butter in a small pan, add the flour and cook over a gentle heat for 2–3 minutes. Add the milk, a little at a time, stirring well. Bring to the boil, then simmer for 3–4 minutes until the sauce is thick.
Flake the smoked haddock and remove any skin and bones. Stir the fish and cheese into the sauce and add salt and pepper to taste.
Roll out the pastry thinly and cut into rounds, using a 7.5 cm/3 inch biscuit cutter. Put a little of the fish mixture on each round of pastry. Dampen the edges and bring them up to make a tricon shape.
Press lightly to seal and put on a baking sheet. Place in a preheated oven and bake for 12–15 minutes until golden brown. Serve hot, or cool on a wire tray and serve cold.
Keeps up to 1 day stored in the refrigerator.
Makes 20–24

PASTRY SAVOURIES

Anchovy canapés

Preparation time: 30 minutes, plus chilling
Cooking time: 10 minutes
Oven: 200°C, 400°F, Gas Mark 6

Metric
100 g Cheese Pastry
 (page 7)
75 g butter
1½ × 5 ml spoons anchovy
 essence
freshly ground black
 pepper
18 anchovy fillets
18 stuffed green olives

Imperial
4 oz Cheese Pastry
 (page 7)
3 oz butter
1½ teaspoons anchovy
 essence
freshly ground black
 pepper
18 anchovy fillets
18 stuffed green olives

Roll out the cheese pastry 5 mm/¼ inch thick. Cut into rounds, using a 4 cm/1½ inch biscuit cutter. Put on a baking sheet. Place in a preheated oven and bake for about 10 minutes or until golden brown. Cool on a wire tray.

Cream the butter until soft and beat in the anchovy essence. Season with black pepper to taste. Either spread this on the cold biscuits with a knife, or put the butter mixture in a piping bag fitted with a medium rosette nozzle and pipe a star of the anchovy butter on each one.

Cut the anchovy fillets in half lengthways and cut the stuffed olives across in half. Wrap an anchovy fillet around each olive half and press on to the savour butter on each canapé. Chill before serving.

Pastry bases keep up to 10 days in an airtight tin. When completed, eat on the same day.

Makes 36

42

Spicy cheese canapés

Metric	Imperial
100 g Cheese Pastry (page 7)	4 oz Cheese Pastry (page 7)
100 g full fat soft cheese	4 oz full fat soft cheese
1 × 5 ml spoon creamed horseradish sauce	1 teaspoon creamed horseradish sauce
salt	salt
freshly ground white pepper	freshly ground white pepper
18 grapes, halved and seeded	18 grapes, halved and seeded

Preparation time: 30 minutes
Cooking time: 10 minutes
Oven: 200°C, 400°F, Gas Mark 6

Prepare and bake the cheese biscuits as for Anchovy Canapés (opposite).
Sieve the cheese and flavour to taste with the creamed horseradish, salt and pepper. When the biscuits are cold, pile the mixture on top and garnish them with a grape half.
Pastry bases keep up to 10 days in an airtight tin. When completed, eat on the same day.
Makes 36

Blue cheese canapés

Metric	Imperial
100 g Cheese Pastry (page 7)	4 oz Cheese Pastry (page 7)
100 g blue cheese	4 oz blue cheese
100 g butter	4 oz butter
2 × 5 ml spoons milk	2 teaspoons milk
freshly ground black pepper	freshly ground black pepper
about 40 g hazelnuts, to garnish	about 1½ oz hazelnuts, to garnish

Preparation time: 30 minutes, plus chilling
Cooking time: 10 minutes
Oven: 200°C, 400°F, Gas Mark 6

Stilton, Danish Blue, Gorgonzola or Roquefort are among the blue cheeses suitable to use for these canapés. They can be made in rounds, or varied by cutting squares, triangles with a knife, or fancy shapes using special cutters.

Prepare and bake the cheese biscuits as for Anchovy Canapés (opposite).
Sieve the cheese with the butter, adding a little milk to give a creamy consistency. Add black pepper to taste and beat well.
Put the hazelnuts on a grill pan and brown under the grill, shaking them frequently to brown evenly. Put on a clean tea towel and rub to remove the skins.
When the biscuits are cold, put the cheese butter in a piping bag filled with a star nozzle and use this to decorate each biscuit. Press a skinned, browned hazelnut on each one. Chill before serving.
Pastry bases keep up to 10 days in an airtight tin. When completed, eat on the same day.
Makes 30–36

Anchovy canapés; Spicy cheese canapés; Blue cheese canapés

Cheese dartois

Metric	Imperial
100 g Flaky or Puff Pastry (pages 8 and 9), chilled	*4 oz Flaky or Puff Pastry (pages 8 and 9), chilled*
75 g cheese, grated	*3 oz cheese, grated*
salt	*salt*
freshly ground white pepper	*freshly ground white pepper*
1 egg, beaten	*1 egg, beaten*

Preparation time: 15 minutes
Cooking time: 20 minutes
Oven: 220°C, 425°F, Gas Mark 7

These can be made with puff or flaky pastry. When you bake with either of these pastries, there are often trimmings left over. Re-roll these, keeping them in the layers, and they will be suitable for this recipe.

Roll out the pastry to a 30 cm/12 inch square. Cut into four 7.5 cm/3 inch strips. Cover 2 of these with grated cheese and season with a little salt and pepper. Place another piece of pastry on each one. Press down lightly and cut into 2.5 cm/1 inch pieces.
Brush with beaten egg and mark with a line down the centre and a chevron pattern each side of it. Put on a baking sheet. Place in a preheated oven and bake for 15 minutes. Cool on a wire rack.
Keeps up to 4 days in an airtight tin.
Makes 24

Savoury cornets

Metric	Imperial
100 g Flaky Pastry (page 8), chilled	*4 oz Flaky Pastry (page 8), chilled*
1 egg, beaten	*1 egg, beaten*
225 g full fat soft cheese	*8 oz full fat soft cheese*
1 × 15 ml spoon strained sauce from mango chutney	*1 tablespoon strained sauce from mango chutney*
1 × 2.5 ml spoon curry powder	*½ teaspoon curry powder*
little red pimento, to garnish	*little red pimento, to garnish*

Aigrettes au fromage

Metric	Imperial
90 g cheese, finely grated	*3½ oz cheese, finely grated*
pinch of cayenne	*pinch of cayenne*
salt	*salt*
freshly ground black pepper	*freshly ground black pepper*
65 g Choux Pastry (page 10)	*2½ oz Choux Pastry (page 10)*

Preparation time: 10 minutes
Cooking time: 20–25 minutes

Mix 50 g/2 oz of the grated cheese, the cayenne, salt and pepper into the choux pastry.
Heat the oil or fat in a deep fat pan. Carefully drop small spoonfuls of the mixture into the hot fat, leaving room for them to rise. Cook for 7–8 minutes, turning occasionally until crisp and golden brown. Remove from the pan with a draining spoon and place on a baking sheet covered with paper towels to drain off any excess fat. Keep hot, uncovered.
Pile on to a heated serving dish and sprinkle with the remaining grated cheese.
Eat immediately, or keep in a warm oven for 30 minutes.
Makes 25–30

Preparation time: 30 minutes
Cooking time: 10–12 minutes
Oven: 220°C, 425°F, Gas Mark 7

Roll out the pastry thinly to a 20 × 25 cm/8 × 10 inch rectangle. Cut down the shorter length into 1 cm/½ inch strips.
Make small cornets in the same way as Cream Horns (page 31). Place on a dampened baking sheet and brush with beaten egg. Place in a preheated oven and bake for 10–12 minutes. Cool on a wire tray.
Meanwhile, mix the cream cheese, mango chutney sauce and curry powder together. Put into a piping bag fitted with a small star nozzle. Fill the cornets with the cheese mixture and garnish the top of each with a small square of red pimento.
Empty cases keep up to 10 days in an airtight tin. Reheat before using.
Makes 20

From the back, clockwise: Aigrettes au fromage; Cheese dartois; Savoury cornets

PIES AND FLANS

Pies and flans have a universal appeal for all occasions. They range from the homely fruit pie to elaborate continental fruit and cream flans. The textures of the pastries, short, sweet or flaky, and the flavours of the fillings enable the hostess to provide a contrast with the other courses in the meal she is serving. Several recipes use 'baked blind' flan cases; the pastry cases are baked in advance, ready to fill and decorate quickly when they are needed – so time-saving when entertaining.

Apple and orange flan

Metric
100 g Shortcrust Pastry
 (page 6)

Imperial
4 oz Shortcrust Pastry
 (page 6)

Filling:
grated rind and juice of 1
 orange
1 large cooking apple,
 peeled, cored and sliced
75 g brown sugar
1 × 1.25 ml spoon ground
 ginger
2 egg yolks

Filling:
grated rind and juice of 1
 orange
1 large cooking apple,
 peeled, cored and sliced
3 oz brown sugar
¼ teaspoon ground
 ginger
2 egg yolks

To decorate:
2 oranges, peeled, or
 1 × 300 g can
 mandarin oranges,
 drained

To decorate:
2 oranges, peeled, or
 1 × 11 oz can
 mandarin oranges,
 drained

Preparation time: 30 minutes
Cooking time: 45 minutes
Oven: 190°C, 375°F, Gas Mark 5;
 160°C, 325°F, Gas Mark 3

Roll out the pastry into a circle and use to line an 18 cm/7 inch flan ring. Place in a preheated oven and bake blind for 20 minutes. Remove the greaseproof paper and beans and return to the oven for 5 minutes to dry the base.
Place the orange rind in a saucepan with the apple, 2 × 15 ml spoons/2 tablespoons of the orange juice, the brown sugar and ginger. Simmer until the apple forms a purée, then leave to cool.
Beat the egg yolks into the apple purée, and pour into the baked flan case. Reduce the oven temperature, place the flan in the oven for 20 minutes or until set. Remove from the flan ring and cool on a wire tray. Cut the oranges into segments or use canned mandarins and decorate the flan.
Empty case keeps up to 4 days. When filled, eat on the same day.
Serves 4–6

Peach flan

Metric
100 g Shortcrust Pastry
 (page 6)
1 × 425 g can sliced
 peaches, drained
1 × 5 ml spoon arrowroot

Imperial
4 oz Shortcrust Pastry
 (page 6)
1 × 15 oz can sliced
 peaches, drained
1 teaspoon arrowroot

To decorate:
3–4 glacé cherries
crystallized angelica

To decorate:
3–4 glacé cherries
crystallized angelica

Preparation time: 20 minutes, plus cooling
Cooking time: 25 minutes
Oven: 200°C, 400°F, Gas Mark 6;
 180°C, 350°F, Gas Mark 4

This flan is made with an edge strengthened with another layer of pastry, giving the advantage of thin pastry on the base with thicker sides which will not break with the moist filling.

Roll out the pastry until it is about 4 cm/1½ inches wider than an 18 cm/7 inch flan ring. Line the flan ring with the pastry and, with the rolling pin, roll across the top of the flan to cut off the excess.
Lightly dampen the inside edge of the flan and re-line this edge with the remaining pastry. Trim off the top with a sharp knife so that the two layers are joined. Place in a preheated oven and bake blind for 20 minutes. If the pastry starts to brown rapidly, reduce the oven temperature and cook until the pastry is lightly coloured.
Remove the greaseproof paper and beans and return to the oven for 5 minutes to dry the base. Remove the flan ring and cool on a wire tray.
Arrange the peaces overlapping closely in a circle in the bottom of the flan. Fill the centre with neatly chopped or half slices of peaches. Blend the arrowroot with a little water.
Heat 150 ml/¼ pint of the canned peach syrup in a pan, add the arrowroot and bring to the boil, stirring continuously. Pour over the peaches and allow to cool. Decorate with halved glacé cherries and small leaves cut from the angelica.
Empty case keeps up to 4 days. When filled, eat on the same day.
Serves 5–6

Peach flan; Apple and orange flan

Damson puff pie

Metric	Imperial
225 g Puff Pastry (page 9) or 1 × 375 g packet frozen puff pastry, thawed	8 oz Puff Pastry (page 9) or 1 × 13 oz packet frozen puff pastry, thawed
pinch of salt	pinch of salt
beaten egg	beaten egg
225 g damsons	8 oz damsons
2 × 15 ml spoons raspberry jam	2 tablespoons raspberry jam
little icing sugar	little icing sugar

Preparation time: 20 minutes
Cooking time: 30–35 minutes
Oven 220°C, 425°F, Gas Mark 7;
    200°C, 400°F, Gas Mark 6

Other combinations of plums and jams can also be good – greengages with apricot jam for instance. Frozen fruit can be used instead of fresh.

Roll out the pastry into a rectangle 40 × 20 cm/16 × 8 inches. Cut in half to give two 20 cm/8 inch squares. Cut a triangular piece off each corner to leave an octagonal shape. Add the salt to the beaten eggs. Brush the top edge of 1 piece of pastry with beaten egg. Stir the fruit and jam together, coating the fruit completely. Spread in the centre of the pastry, leaving a 2.5 cm/1 inch border.
On the second piece of pastry cut a cross to within 4 cm/1½ inches of the edge; lift this piece on to the pie and press the edges neatly together, knock up and flute the edges. Brush the top of the pie with beaten egg and open the centre cut, turning and pressing back the pastry to show the fruit filling.
Lift the pie on to a dampened baking sheet, place on the top shelf of a preheated oven and bake for 20 minutes. Remove the pie from the oven and reduce the oven temperature.
Sift a layer of icing sugar over the top and quickly return to the oven for a further 10–15 minutes. If the filling should start to bubble over or the pastry becomes too brown, reduce the oven temperature once again.
Keeps up to 2 days.
Serves 4–6

Caribbean flan

Metric	Imperial
175 g Shortcrust Pastry (page 6)	6 oz Shortcrust Pastry (page 6)
50 g plain flour	2 oz plain flour
1 × 2.5 ml spoon baking powder	½ teaspoon baking powder
50 g caster sugar	2 oz caster sugar
50 g soft margarine or softened butter	2 oz soft margarine or softened butter
1 egg	1 egg
25 g fine desiccated coconut	1 oz fine desiccated coconut
grated rind of 2 oranges	grated rind of 2 oranges
3 bananas	3 bananas
40 g butter	1½ oz butter
50 g demerara sugar	2 oz demerara sugar
150 ml orange juice	¼ pint orange juice
juice of ½ lemon	juice of ½ lemon

Preparation time: 25 minutes
Cooking time: 30 minutes
Oven: 190°C, 375°F, Gas Mark 5

Roll out the pastry into a circle and use to line a 22 cm/8½ inch flan ring. Sift the flour, baking powder and sugar into a bowl, add the margarine or butter, egg, desiccated coconut and orange rind.
Beat the ingredients together until the mixture is light and fluffy. Fill the pastry case with this sponge mixture. Place in a preheated oven and bake for about 30 minutes until a light golden brown. Remove from the flan ring.
Cut the bananas into 5 mm/¼ inch thick slices. Heat the butter in a frying pan, toss the bananas in the demerara sugar and fry quickly over a moderate heat until lightly coloured on both sides. Arrange closely in circles on top of the sponge.
Pour the orange and lemon juice into the frying pan and boil until 3–4 × 15 ml spoons/3–4 tablespoons remain. Pour over the bananas and serve hot or cold.
Keeps up to 2 days.
Serves 6–8

From the back: Caribbean flan; Damson puff pie

Pineapple and cottage cheese flan

Metric	Imperial
100 g Shortcrust Pastry (page 6)	4 oz Shortcrust Pastry (page 6)
175 g cottage cheese	6 oz cottage cheese
120 ml double or whipping cream	4 fl oz double or whipping cream
2 × 5 ml spoons powdered gelatine	2 teaspoons powdered gelatine
2 × 15 ml spoons water	2 tablespoons water
1 egg white	1 egg white
1 × 15 ml spoon lemon juice	1 tablespoon lemon juice
1 × 225 g can pineapple slices	1 × 8 oz can pineapple slices
few glacé cherries	few glacé cherries
crystallized angelica	crystallized angelica
1 × 5 ml spoon arrowroot	1 teaspoon arrowroot

Preparation time: 35 minutes, plus setting
Cooking time: 25 minutes
Oven: 190°C, 375°F, Gas Mark 5

Roll out the pastry into a circle and use to line an 18 cm/7 inch flan ring. Place in a preheated oven and bake blind for 20 minutes. Remove the greaseproof paper and beans and return to the oven for 5 minutes to dry. Remove from the flan ring and cool on a wire tray. Sieve the cottage cheese into a bowl, add the cream and beat together. Put the gelatine in a heatproof bowl with the water. Allow to soak for 5 minutes, then place over a pan of warm water to dissolve, stirring occasionally. Meanwhile, whisk the egg white until stiff and standing in peaks. Stir the dissolved gelatine and the lemon juice into the cheese mixture, then fold in the egg white. Spoon into the flan case and smooth the top. Leave to set.

Drain the pineapple and reserve the juice. Cut the pineapple into thin slices or segments. Arrange on top in a decorative pattern with halved glacé cherries and leaves of angelica. Blend the arrowroot with a little of the canned pineapple juice. Bring the remaining pineapple juice to the boil and pour on to the arrowroot. Return to the pan and bring to the boil, stirring. Cool slightly and use to glaze the flan. Serve the flan cold.

Empty case keeps up to 4 days in an airtight tin. When filled, eat on the same day.
Serves 5–6

Variations:
Substitute fresh strawberries for the pineapple slices, and glaze the fruit with hot redcurrant jelly.
Substitute fresh pineapple for canned, and glaze with sieved hot apricot jam.

Treacle tart

Metric	Imperial
100 g Shortcrust Pastry (page 6)	4 oz Shortcrust Pastry (page 6)
6 × 15 ml spoons white breadcrumbs	6 tablespoons white breadcrumbs
6 × 15 ml spoons golden syrup	6 tablespoons golden syrup
grated rind and juice of ½ lemon	grated rind and juice of ½ lemon

Preparation time: 15 minutes
Cooking time: 40–45 minutes
Oven: 180°C, 350°F, Gas Mark 4

Roll out the pastry thinly into a circle and use to line a 23 cm/9 inch ovenproof plate. Trim and flute the edge. Roll out the trimmings and make leaves or small circles. Brush the back of them with water and arrange decoratively around the flat edge of the plate. Mix together the breadcrumbs, golden syrup and grated lemon rind and juice. Pour on to the pastry and smooth out so that the mixture covers the base of the plate. Place in a preheated oven and bake for 40–45 minutes. Serve hot or cold.
Keeps up to 4 days.
Serves 4–6

Variations:
Use 4 × 15 ml spoons/4 tablespoons porridge oats or wholemeal breadcrumbs instead of white breadcrumbs. Wholemeal pastry can also be used.

Yorkshire curd tart

Metric
175 g Shortcrust Pastry
   (page 6)
225 g curd or cottage
   cheese
2 eggs, lightly beaten
50 g currants
pinch of grated nutmeg
grated rind of ½ lemon
75 g sugar
25 g butter, melted and
   cooled

Imperial
6 oz Shortcrust Pastry
   (page 6)
8 oz curd or cottage
   cheese
2 eggs, lightly beaten
2 oz currants
pinch of grated nutmeg
grated rind of ½ lemon
3 oz sugar
1 oz butter, melted and
   cooled

Preparation time: 20 minutes
Cooking time: 1 hour
Oven: 190°C, 375°F, Gas Mark 5;
   180°C, 350°F, Gas Mark 4

Yorkshire is famous for its cheese tarts. This one is delicately spiced and can be served as a pudding or at teatime, sprinkled with a little icing sugar.

Roll out the pastry into a circle and use to line a 22 cm/8½ inch deep pie plate. Trim, knock up and flute the edge.
Sieve the cheese into a bowl and beat in the eggs, currants, nutmeg, lemon rind, sugar and melted butter. Stir well and pour into the pastry case.
Place in a preheated oven and bake for 30 minutes, then reduce the oven temperature and continue cooking for a further 30 minutes or until set and a pale golden brown.
Keeps up to 2 days.
Serves 5–6

From the left: Treacle tart; Yorkshire curd tart;
Pineapple and cottage cheese flan

Coffee chiffon pie

Metric
100 g Rich Shortcrust
  Pastry (page 7)
15 g powdered gelatine
75 ml water
300 ml milk
4 × 5 ml spoons instant
  coffee powder
65 g sugar
2 eggs, separated
150 ml double or
  whipping cream,
  lightly whipped

To decorate:
75 ml double or
  whipping cream, stiffly
  whipped
few walnut halves

Imperial
4 oz Rich Shortcrust
  Pastry (page 7)
½ oz powdered gelatine
2½ fl oz water
½ pint milk
4 teaspoons instant coffee
  powder
2½ oz sugar
2 eggs, separated
¼ pint double or
  whipping cream,
  lightly whipped

To decorate:
2½ fl oz double or
  whipping cream, stiffly
  whipped
few walnut halves

Preparation time: 45 minutes
Cooking time: 20–25 minutes
Oven: 190°C, 375°F, Gas Mark 5

Crisp rich shortcrust pastry and a light fluffy mousse make a pleasing combination for this pie.

Roll out the pastry into a circle and use to line a 22 cm/8½ inch deep pie plate. Trim and flute the edge. Place in a preheated oven and bake blind for 20 minutes. Remove the greaseproof paper and beans and return to the oven for 5 minutes to dry the base. Allow to cool.
Put the gelatine in a small heatproof bowl with the water, allow to soak for 5 minutes, then place over a pan of hot water to dissolve, stirring occasionally.
Heat the milk and coffee together until just below boiling. Add the sugar to the egg yolks and beat until thoroughly blended. Pour the hot milk on to the egg mixture and stir well, then return the custard to the pan and cook over a gentle heat until it thickens slightly. The custard will just coat the back of a metal spoon when thick enough.
Add the dissolved gelatine to the custard. Strain into a large clean pan and leave to cool.
When the custard is on the point of setting, whisk the egg whites stiffly and fold the cream and then the egg whites into the custard. Pour into the cold pastry case and allow to set.
To decorate, spoon the cream into a piping bag fitted with a large star nozzle and pipe the edge of the pie with stars of cream. Decorate with the walnut halves and serve cold.
Empty case keeps up to 4 days. When filled, eat on the same day.
Serves 6–8

Butterscotch pear flan

Metric
100 g Shortcrust Pastry
  (page 6)
2 × 15 ml spoons
  cornflour
300 ml milk
25 g butter
50 g sugar
25 g walnuts, coarsely
  chopped
1 × 400 g can pear halves
2 × 15 ml spoons apricot
  jam

Imperial
4 oz Shortcrust Pastry
  (page 6)
2 tablespoons cornflour
½ pint milk
1 oz butter
2 oz sugar
1 oz walnuts, coarsely
  chopped
1 × 14 oz can pear
  halves
2 tablespoons apricot
  jam

Preparation time: 20 minutes
Cooking time: 25 minutes
Oven: 190°C, 375°F, Gas Mark 5

The butterscotch flavoured filling is made by caramelizing butter and sugar.

Roll out the pastry into a circle and use to line an 18 cm/7 inch flan ring. Place in a preheated oven and bake blind for 20 minutes. Remove the greaseproof paper and beans and return to the oven for 5 minutes to dry the base. Allow to cool slightly, remove from the flan ring and cool on a wire tray.
Put the cornflour in a bowl with a little of the milk and blend together. Warm the remaining milk in a saucepan.
Melt the butter in a fairly large saucepan, add the sugar and stir until melted. Boil until golden brown. Pour the warm milk on to the sugar and butter mixture; at this stage it will boil vigorously, so lift the pan off the heat for a moment. Stir until the butterscotch is dissolved.
Pour the flavoured milk on to the cornflour, stir well and return to the pan. Bring to the boil, stirring continuously, and simmer for about 2 minutes. Pour into the pastry case and sprinkle the top with walnuts. Allow to cool.
Drain the pears and arrange on top of the flan. Boil and sieve the apricot jam and brush over the pears to glaze. Serve cold.
Empty case keeps up to 4 days. When filled, eat on the same day.
Serves 5–6

From the back left, clockwise: Coffee chiffon pie;
Butterscotch pear flan; Moka fudge flan

Moka fudge flan

Preparation time: 20 minutes
Cooking time: 25 minutes
Oven: 190°C, 375°F, Gas Mark 5

Metric
100 g Shortcrust Pastry
(page 6)

Filling:
225 g plain chocolate,
broken into pieces
2 × 5 ml spoons instant
coffee powder
1 × 15 ml spoon boiling
water
50 g butter, cut into
pieces
2 egg yolks
1 × 15 ml spoon double
cream
few walnut halves, to
decorate

Imperial
4 oz Shortcrust Pastry
(page 6)

Filling:
8 oz plain chocolate,
broken into pieces
1 teaspoon instant coffee
powder
1 tablespoon boiling
water
2 oz butter, cut into
pieces
2 egg yolks
1 tablespoon double
cream
few walnut halves, to
decorate

Roll out the pastry into a circle and use to line an 18 cm/7 inch flan tin. Place in a preheated oven and bake blind for 20 minutes. Remove the greaseproof paper and beans and return to the oven for 5 minutes to dry the base. Allow to cool slightly, remove from the flan tin and cool on a wire tray.

Meanwhile, place the chocolate pieces in a bowl, put over a pan of warm water and allow the chocolate to melt. Dissolve the instant coffee in the boiling water and blend into the melted chocolate. Remove from the heat and stir in the butter, piece by piece. Stir in the egg yolks and cream. Spoon into the flan case and swirl the top into a pattern. Decorate with the walnut halves. Chill before serving.

Empty case keeps up to 4 days. When filled, eat within 2 days.

Serves 6

Apricot meringue

Metric	Imperial
225 g dried apricots, soaked overnight (see method)	8 oz dried apricots, soaked overnight (see method)
600 ml boiling water	1 pint boiling water
50 g sugar	2 oz sugar
2 eggs, separated	2 eggs, separated
100 g Shortcrust Pastry (page 6)	4 oz Shortcrust Pastry (page 6)

Meringue:	Meringue:
100 g caster sugar	4 oz caster sugar
little icing sugar	little icing sugar

Preparation time: 35 minutes, plus soaking
Cooking time: 1 hour 5 minutes
Oven: 200°C, 400°F, Gas Mark 6;
      150°C, 300°F, Gas Mark 2

Cover the apricots with the boiling water and leave to soak overnight or for at least 2 hours. Simmer the apricots in the soaking water until they are tender. The cooking time will depend on how long they have been soaked – about 20 minutes if they have been soaked overnight, or up to 1 hour if soaked for a few hours only. When tender, boil to reduce most of the liquid. Add the sugar and stir over a gentle heat until the sugar has dissolved. Continue cooking, stirring continuously, until the mixture is thick.

Remove from the heat and allow to cool slightly. Either pass the apricot mixture through a vegetable mill and beat the egg yolks into the purée or place the apricot mixture and egg yolks in a blender and liquidize.

Roll out the pastry into a circle and use to line an 18 cm/7 inch flan ring. Place in a preheated oven and bake blind. Remove the greaseproof paper and baking beans and return to the oven for 5 minutes to dry the base. Fill the flan case with the apricot mixture and return to the oven for 10 minutes.

Whisk the egg whites until stiff. Add 1 × 15 ml/1 tablespoon of the caster sugar and beat until the mixture is stiff, then gently fold in the remaining sugar in 2 or 3 batches.

Either pipe the meringue on to the top of the flan using a piping bag fitted with a large star nozzle, or swirl over the top, lifting it into peaks using the back of a spoon. Sift a little icing sugar over the top.

Reduce the oven temperature, and bake the flan for 30 minutes.

Empty case keeps up to 4 days in an airtight tin. When filled, eat within 24 hours.

Serves 5–6

Tarte aux poires au vin rouge

Preparation time: 35 minutes, plus cooling
Cooking time: 25 minutes
Oven: 190°C, 375°F, Gas Mark 5

Metric	Imperial
150 g Pâte Sucrée (page 8)	*5 oz Pâte Sucrée (page 8)*
7 small pears, peeled and halved	*7 small pears, peeled and halved*
75 g sugar	*3 oz sugar*
300 ml red wine	*½ pint red wine*
150 ml water	*¼ pint water*
1 × 15 ml spoon redcurrant jelly	*1 tablespoon redcurrant jelly*
1 × 15 ml spoon seedless raspberry jam	*1 tablespoon seedless raspberry jam*

To decorate:
150 ml double or whipping cream, stiffly whipped
few flaked almonds, browned

To decorate:
¼ pint double or whipping cream, stiffly whipped
few flaked almonds, browned

Pears cooked in red wine are a great favourite in France and this variation makes a delicious and colourful flan. For best results, choose a red wine you would be happy to drink and pears which are a good round shape. Small William pears are excellent. Conference pears can be too long to fit into the pastry case, but if they are the only ones available, the stalk ends can be trimmed and rounded to make them fit.

Roll out the pastry into a circle and use to line a 22 cm/8½ inch flan ring. Place in a preheated oven and bake blind for 20 minutes. Remove the greaseproof paper and beans and return to the oven for 5 minutes to dry the base. Remove the flan ring and cool on a wire tray.

Scoop out the pear cores neatly with a small teaspoon or a ball cutter and remove the threads of the stalks. Slice the pears thinly.

Dissolve the sugar in the wine and water over a gentle heat in a shallow pan with a lid; a frying pan is ideal for this. Bring the syrup to the boil, then add the sliced pears. Cover and cook gently until tender.

Remove the pear slices from the pan, draining well and returning any syrup to the pan.

Arrange the sliced pears in a neat layer in the flan case. Add the redcurrant jelly and the raspberry jam to the syrup and stir over a low heat until dissolved. Bring to the boil without stirring and boil until the liquid is thick, syrupy and of a coating consistency. (Great care is needed at this stage as it is important to reduce the syrup sufficiently so that it will just coat the pears. If it is too thin it runs out of the tart, if it is too thick, it will set too firmly.) Pour the syrup over the pears and leave to cool completely.

Spoon the whipped cream into a piping bag with a star nozzle and pipe swirls around the edge of the flan. Sprinkle the cream with a few crushed flaked almonds and serve cold.

Empty case keeps up to 4 days in an airtight tin. When filled, eat on the same day.

Serves 6

Apricot meringue; Tarte aux poires au vin rouge

PETITS FOURS

A plate of small delicious looking petits fours served with coffee after dinner can be a luxurious and perfect ending to a meal. They can be served at a wedding reception, or a special tea party or coffee morning when they will be immensely popular. If you make 2 or 3 varieties, arrange them together on platters so that everyone can choose their favourites. Petits fours with a sponge cake base, such as sponge finger biscuits need to be freshly made, but the crisp little biscuits like Tuiles aux Noisettes or Almond Leaves can be made at least a week ahead, providing they are stored in airtight containers. For fund raising events, pack them in cling-film-wrapped food trays.

Genoese sponge

Metric	*Imperial*
25 g butter	*1 oz butter*
2 eggs	*2 eggs*
65 g caster sugar	*2½ oz caster sugar*
50 g plain flour, sifted	*2 oz plain flour, sifted*

Preparation time: 20 minutes
Cooking time: 35–40 minutes
Oven: 180°C, 350°F, Gas Mark 4

Place the butter in a bowl, standing over a bowl of water and heat for a few minutes until the butter melts, but does not become hot.
Beat the eggs and sugar together in a bowl, then place over a saucepan of very hot water. Beat until the mixture becomes thick and creamy, and leaves a trail when a little of the mixture is pulled across the surface. Remove from the heat and beat until the mixture is cold.
Fold in the flour in about 3 batches, alternately with the melted butter.
Pour into a greased and floured 18 cm/7 inch square tin. Place in a preheated oven and bake for 35–40 minutes or until the sponge is golden brown, firm to the touch and begins to shrink from the side of the tin.
Remove from the tin and cool on a wire tray.
Keeps up to 7 days in an airtight tin.
Makes one 18 cm/7 inch square cake

Chocolate boxes

Metric	**Imperial**
165 g chocolate, broken in pieces	5 oz chocolate, broken in pieces
1 quantity Genoese Sponge (opposite)	1 quantity Genoese Sponge (opposite)
1 quantity Chocolate Crème au Beurre Mousseline (right)	1 quantity Chocolate Crème au Beurre Mousseline (right)

Preparation time: 30 minutes

Place the chocolate pieces in a bowl, standing over a bowl of hot water. Fasten a piece of greaseproof paper to a pastry board or baking sheet with adhesive tape. Pour the melted chocolate on to the paper and, with a palette knife, spread it thinly to cover a 30 cm/12 inch square. When set, trim off the uneven edges and mark the chocolate into 4 cm/1½ inch squares.

Trim the edges from the sponge and cut into 4 even strips. Cut each one in half horizontally and spread with a little Chocolate Crème au Beurre Mousseline. Reform the strips and cut each one into four. Spread a little of the Crème au Beurre over the sides and top of each square.

Taking care to handle the chocolate as little as possible, press one square of chocolate against the sides of each piece of sponge to form a neat box.

Put the remaining butter cream in a paper piping bag filled with a fine small star nozzle and pipe 3 lines of 3 stars on the top of each box. Place each one in a paper case to serve.

Keeps up to 3 days.

Makes 16

Crème au beurre mousseline

Metric	**Imperial**
35 g sugar	1¼ oz sugar
4 × 15 ml spoons water	4 tablespoons water
1 egg yolk	1 egg yolk
65 g unsalted butter, cut in small pieces	2½ oz unsalted butter, cut in small pieces

Preparation time: 5 minutes
Cooking time: about 25 minutes

Crème au Beurre Mousseline can be flavoured to taste with liqueurs, essences, the grated rind and juice of oranges or lemons (see below), or melted chocolate.

Place the sugar and water in a small saucepan and heat gently, stirring occasionally, until the sugar has dissolved. Bring to the boil, but do not stir again. Boil until the temperature reaches 103°C/215°F.

To test without a thermometer, dip the thumb or forefinger first into cold water and then quickly in and out of the boiling sugar. The water acts as an insulation, but the fingers must be dipped into cold water every time the sugar is tested. The sugar has reached the correct temperature when a fine thread is formed when the finger and thumb are pulled apart. While the syrup is boiling, beat the egg yolk. When the thread stage is reached, quickly pour the syrup on to the egg yolk and beat until light and fluffy. Beat in the butter, a piece at a time. If the mixture curdles, beat in a little more butter. Add flavourings, if used. Can be made 2–3 days in advance. If it becomes firm and difficult to spread, stand it in a bowl over warm water until it starts to soften, then beat until smooth.

Makes about 100 g/4 oz

Flavourings:
You will need to use about 1 × 15 ml spoon/1 tablespoon liqueur or fruit juice, or a few drops of essence for flavouring.

To flavour with chocolate, melt 50 g/2 oz chocolate in a bowl, standing over a bowl of hot water. When the chocolate is liquid and smooth, beat it into the Crème au Beurre Mousseline. Leave in a cool place to set.

Genoese sponge; Crème au beurre mousseline; Chocolate boxes

Italiens

Metric	Imperial
1 quantity Genoese Sponge (page 56)	1 quantity Genoese Sponge (page 56)
1 quantity Crème au Beurre Mousseline (page 57)	1 quantity Crème au Beurre Mousseline (page 57)
2 × 15 ml spoons Kirsch or few drops of almond essence	2 tablespoons Kirsch or few drops of almond essence

To finish:	To finish:
350 g icing sugar, sifted	12 oz icing sugar, sifted
3 × 15 ml spoons water	3 tablespoons water
little green food colouring	little green food colouring
10 blanched almonds	10 blanched almonds

Preparation time: 20 minutes

Trim the edges from the sponge and cut into 4 strips. Cut each one in half lengthways. Mix the Crème au Beurre Mousseline with the Kirsch or almond essence and spread a layer on each strip of sponge. Reform and place on a wire tray.

Put the remaining butter cream in a piping bag fitted with a 1 cm/½ inch plain nozzle. Pipe a band of the cream down the length of each strip. Place in the refrigerator to become firm.

Put the icing sugar in a bowl, standing over a saucepan of hot water, and mix with sufficient water to give a coating consistency. Add a little green food colouring. Stir well until smooth. Pour the icing over each sponge strip, making certain the sides as well as the top are coated with icing. Put a plate under the wire tray to catch the surplus icing.

Split the almonds in half and place 5 evenly on top of each band. Dip a knife into hot water and diagonally cut each strip between each nut. Put into paper cases to serve.

Keeps for 1 day.

Makes 20

Friandises

Metric	Imperial
450 g sugar	1 lb sugar
50 g powdered glucose	2 oz powdered glucose
150 ml water	¼ pint water
450 g prepared mixed fruit, e.g. 225 g strawberries, 100 black grapes, 2 oranges	1 lb prepared mixed fruit, e.g. 8 oz strawberries, 4 oz black grapes, 2 oranges

Preparation time: 15 minutes
Cooking time: 30 minutes

These sugared fruits are delightful to eat and will certainly impress your guests. Dessert gooseberries, cherries, tangerine segments or any other small firm dry fruits can also be used. Make them only 1–2 hours before you want to eat them, keep in a dry place as the sugar coating soon melts, particularly if the atmosphere is damp.

Put the sugar, glucose and water in a saucepan over a gentle heat. Stir until the sugar is dissolved. Bring to the boil without stirring and cook until the syrup reaches hard crack stage 143°C/190°F or until a little of the syrup when dropped into cold water sets firm enough to break crisply. Remove from the heat.

Using 2 forks dipped in oil, dip each piece of fruit into the syrup to coat. Allow the fruit to drain for a moment or two, then place on an oiled baking sheet and leave to set. If the syrup becomes too firm, return to the heat for a short time.

Take particular care not to touch the syrup with the fingers as it is very hot indeed and could cause a painful burn. If the hand is splashed, place it in cold water immediately.

Continue until all the fruit has been dipped and place in small sweet papers to serve.

Add some water to any remaining syrup in the pan, bring to the boil and simmer until the syrup has dissolved. Cool and use for poaching fruit.

Keeps up to 2 hours.

Makes about 50

Printaniers

Preparation time: 20 minutes

Trim the edges from the sponge and cut into 4 strips.
Cut each one in half lengthways. Spread a thin layer of
Crème au Beurre Mousseline on each and reform.
Divide the remainder of the butter cream into three.
Flavour a third with 1–2 drops vanilla essence, colour
one-third pale green and flavour with Kirsch or a little
almond essence. Colour the remaining third of the
mixture pale pink.
With a piping bag(s) fitted with a small star nozzle(s),
pipe a band of each colour down the length of each
strip, covering the top of the sponge completely. Cut
each strip into 5. Put in paper cases to serve.
Keeps for 1 day.
Makes 20

Metric	*Imperial*
Genoese Sponge (page 56)	*Genoese Sponge (page 56)*
Crème au Beurre Mousseline (page 57)	*Crème au Beurre Mousseline (page 57)*
1–2 drops vanilla essence	*1–2 drops vanilla essence*
green and pink food colouring	*green and pink food colouring*
2 × 5 ml spoons Kirsch or few drops of almond essence	*2 teaspoons Kirsch or few drops of almond essence*

From the left: Friandises; Printaniers; Italiens

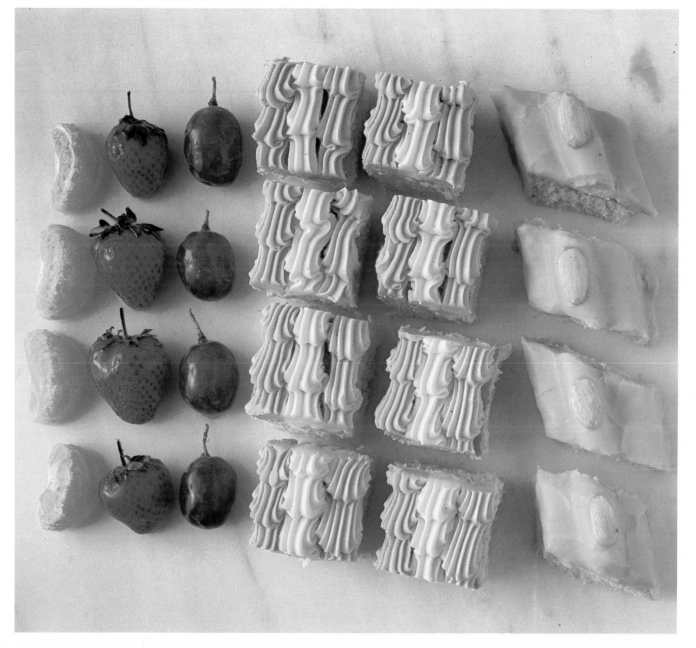

Viscontis

Metric
50 g butter
50 g caster sugar
1 egg, beaten
50 g plain flour, sifted
15 g almonds, chopped

Imperial
2 oz butter
2 oz caster sugar
1 egg, beaten
2 oz plain flour, sifted
½ oz almonds, chopped

Preparation time: about 20 minutes
Cooking time: 8–10 minutes
Oven: 190°C, 375°F, Gas Mark 5

When cold, these crisp little biscuits should be golden brown around the edges, but still pale in the centre. Serve with tea or coffee, or as a crisp accompaniment to a fruit mousse or ice cream. Small ones, shaped into 2.5 cm/1 inch rounds, can be baked to serve with other petits fours with after-dinner coffee.

Cream the butter and sugar together until light and fluffy. Add the egg, a little at a time, beating after each addition. Fold in the flour, half at a time, beating after each addition.
Put small teaspoons of the mixture on 2–3 greased and floured baking sheets; leave plenty of room between them as they spread to about double in size. Place a pinch of chopped nuts on each one. Place in a preheated oven and bake for 8–10 minutes. Cool on a wire tray, taking care to keep them flat.
Keeps up to 4 weeks in an airtight tin.
Makes about 30 × 2.5 cm/1 inch or 20 × 5 cm/2 inch biscuits

Tuiles aux noisettes

Metric
50 g butter
2 egg whites
65 g caster sugar
few drops of vanilla
  essence
50 g flour, sifted
50 g hazelnuts, chopped
little icing sugar

Imperial
2 oz butter
2 egg whites
2½ oz caster sugar
few drops of vanilla
  essence
2 oz flour, sifted
2 oz hazelnuts, chopped
little icing sugar

Preparation time: 10 minutes
Cooking time: 5–6 minutes
Oven: 200°C, 400°F, Gas Mark 6

The name of these biscuits comes from their resemblance to the curved roof tiles that are used a great deal in the south of France. The biscuits are thin and wafer crisp; they are often served with ice cream.

Melt the butter in a saucepan and leave to cool. Whisk the egg whites until thick and frothy. Add the sugar and beat again until thick and white.
Add the vanilla essence to the cool melted butter. Fold the flour into the mixture, about a third at a time, alternating with the melted butter. Fold in the chopped nuts.
Put teaspoons of the mixture on to greased and floured baking sheets, taking care to keep them widely spaced. Spread each one out to a thin 6 cm/2½ inch circle. Sift a little icing sugar over them. Place in a preheated oven and bake for 5–6 minutes until coloured around the edges.
Have a greased rolling pin ready for shaping the tuiles. Place each biscuit on the rolling pin and press it into a curve. This must be done while the biscuits are warm and pliable, as they come from the oven. After shaping, cool on a wire tray.
Keeps up to 4 weeks in an airtight tin.
Makes 20

Iced walnut squares

Metric
3 eggs, separated
100 g caster sugar
100 g walnuts, ground
1 × 5 ml spoon plain
  flour, sifted

To finish:
100 g icing sugar, sifted
2 × 5 ml spoons lemon
  juice
16 walnut halves, to
  decorate

Imperial
3 eggs, separated
4 oz caster sugar
4 oz walnuts, ground
1 teaspoon plain flour,
  sifted

To finish:
4 oz icing sugar, sifted
2 teaspoons lemon
  juice
16 walnut halves, to
  decorate

Preparation time: 30 minutes
Cooking time: 25–30 minutes
Oven: 150°C, 300°F, Gas Mark 2

These iced walnut squares keep well. The cake base can be made and stored in an airtight container and iced a few days later.

Beat the egg yolks with the sugar until thick and light in colour. Stir in the ground walnuts and flour. Whisk the egg whites until stiff and standing in peaks. Fold into the nut mixture.
Spread the mixture into a 20 cm/8 inch greased and floured square deep baking tin. Place in a preheated oven and bake for 25–30 minutes until set and lightly coloured. Remove from the tin and cool on a wire tray. Place the icing sugar in a bowl and stir in sufficient lemon juice to give a smooth consistency. Spread this over the top of the cake. Cut into squares and decorate each one with a walnut half while the icing is still soft. Allow the icing to set before serving.
Uniced cake keeps up to 4 weeks in an airtight tin. When iced, keeps up to 2 weeks.
Makes 16

Viscontis; Tuiles aux noisettes; Iced walnut squares

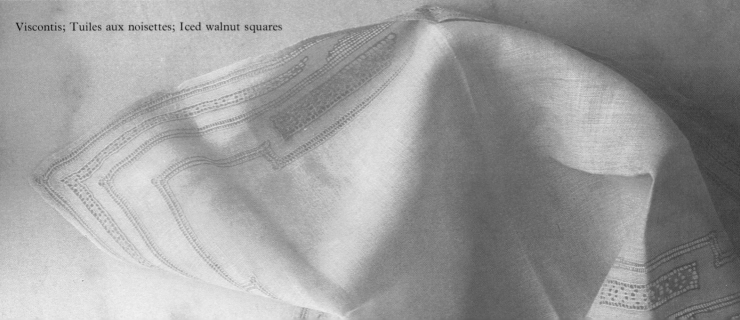

Langues de chat à la crème

Metric
120 ml double cream
120 g icing sugar, sifted
120 g plain flour, sifted
2 egg whites
finely grated rind of 1
   lemon

Imperial
4 fl oz double cream
4½ oz icing sugar, sifted
4½ oz plain flour, sifted
2 egg whites
finely grated rind of 1
   lemon

Preparation time: 20 minutes
Cooking time: 7–8 minutes
Oven: 190°C, 375°F, Gas Mark 5

Place the cream and icing sugar in a bowl and stir together. Add the flour and stir in lightly. Whisk the egg whites until stiff and standing in peaks. Fold a third of the egg white into the mixture at a time. Lightly mix until evenly blended.
Put into a piping bag fitted with a 5 mm/¼ inch or 1 cm/½ inch plain nozzle and pipe in finger lengths on to a greased baking sheet.
As each baking sheet is filled, place in a preheated oven and bake for 7–8 minutes until the mixture is golden brown round the edges, but still pale in the centre. Cool on a wire tray. Keeps up to 4 weeks in an airtight tin.
Makes 50 small or 20 large biscuits

Chocolate balls

Metric
24 hazelnuts
100 g ground almonds
100 g caster sugar
25 g cocoa powder, sifted
1 egg white
50 g granulated sugar

Imperial
24 hazelnuts
4 oz ground almonds
4 oz caster sugar
1 oz cocoa powder, sifted
1 egg white
2 oz granulated sugar

Preparation time: 30 minutes
Cooking time: 10–15 minutes
Oven: 200°C, 400°F, Gas Mark 6

These chocolate almond petits fours have a crisp sugar coating on the outside. They only need a short cooking time – it can be deceptive cooking chocolate coloured biscuits so take care not to overbake as this makes them hard. Should this accidentally happen, leave them exposed to the air for a time and they will become softer.

Brown the hazelnuts under a preheated hot grill, shaking the pan frequently. When the skins split and the nuts are lightly coloured, place them in a clean tea towel and rub to remove the skins, which will fall off very easily.
Place the ground almonds and sugar in a bowl. Add the cocoa powder and mix well. Add sufficient egg white to bind the mixture together to a slightly soft paste.
Divide into portions the size of a walnut and place a hazelnut in the centre of each. Dip first into lightly beaten egg white, then into granulated sugar. Put them on a greased baking sheet. Place in a preheated oven and bake for 10–15 minutes. Cool on a wire tray. Keeps up to 10 days in an airtight tin.
Makes 24

Langues de chat à la crème; Chocolate balls

Ratafias; Doigts des dames

Ratafias

Metric	Imperial
100 g caster sugar	*4 oz caster sugar*
100 g ground almonds	*4 oz ground almonds*
2 egg whites	*2 egg whites*
3–4 drops almond essence	*3–4 drops almond essence*

Preparation time: 20 minutes
Cooking time: 20 minutes
Oven: 140°C, 275°F, Gas Mark 1

These little petits fours were popular in the eight-eenth century in this country. Besides being served as petits fours, they are also useful for decorating fruit trifles.

Put the sugar and ground almonds in a saucepan with the egg whites and almond essence. Beat them thoroughly together. Place over a low heat and cook for 4–5 minutes until the mixture thickens and comes away from the base of the pan.
Spoon the mixture into a piping bag fitted with a 1 cm/½ inch plain nozzle. Pipe the mixture into small rounds on a greased and floured baking sheet. Place in a preheated oven and bake for 20 minutes until set and lightly coloured. Cool on a wire tray.
Keeps up to 3 weeks in an airtight tin.
Makes 15

Doigts des dames

Metric	Imperial
100 g icing sugar, sifted	*4 oz icing sugar, sifted*
2 egg whites	*2 egg whites*
1 × 5 ml spoons instant coffee powder	*1 teaspoon instant coffee powder*
1 × 5 ml spoon boiling water	*1 teaspoon boiling water*

Preparation time: 20 minutes
Cooking time: 8–10 minutes
Oven: 160°C, 325°F, Gas Mark 3

These meringue fingers are crisp on the outer surface, but soft inside.

Place the icing sugar into a large heatproof bowl. Add the egg whites and stir well together. Place the bowl over a saucepan of boiling water and whisk until very thick and white. Remove from the pan and continue beating until stiff and cool. Dissolve the coffee powder in the boiling water and whisk this in, a little at a time, beating until the mixture is thick and glossy.
Place the mixture in a piping bag fitted with a large rosette nozzle and pipe into finger lengths on greased and floured baking sheets. Place in a preheated oven and bake for 8–10 minutes. Cool on a wire tray.
Keeps up to 3 days in an airtight tin.
Makes 20

Almond leaves

Metric	Imperial
45 g butter	$1\frac{3}{4}$ oz butter
120 g caster sugar	$4\frac{1}{2}$ oz caster sugar
120 ground almonds	$4\frac{1}{2}$ oz ground almonds
1 × 5 ml spoon vanilla sugar or few drops of vanilla essence	1 teaspoon vanilla sugar or few drops of vanilla essence
3 egg yolks	3 egg yolks
165 g plain flour, sifted	$5\frac{1}{2}$ oz plain flour, sifted

To finish:

Metric	Imperial
1 egg, beaten	1 egg, beaten
175 g chocolate, broken in pieces	6 oz chocolate, broken in pieces

Preparation time: 40 minutes, plus chilling
Cooking time: 15 minutes
Oven: 180°C, 350°F, Gas Mark 4

Place the butter in a bowl and beat until soft and creamy. Stir in the sugar, ground almonds and vanilla sugar or essence. Add the egg yolks and mix together to a paste. Gradually work all the flour into the mixture. Cover the pastry with cling film or grease-proof paper and chill for 30 minutes.
Roll out the pastry fairly thinly and cut out leaf shapes 5.5 cm/$2\frac{1}{4}$ inch long, using a 6 cm/$2\frac{1}{2}$ inch fluted cutter. Pinch the fluted edges together to form small points. Mark the veining of a leaf on each biscuit with the back of a small knife. Place on a greased baking sheet and brush with beaten egg. Place in a preheated oven and bake for 15 minutes until golden brown. Cool on a wire tray.
Meanwhile, place the chocolate in a bowl, standing over a saucepan of hot water. When melted, dip half of each biscuit into the chocolate. Place on greaseproof paper or cling film until dry.
Keeps up to 4 weeks in an airtight tin.
Makes 30

Rout biscuits

Metric	Imperial
100 g ground almonds	4 oz ground almonds
100 g icing sugar, sifted	4 oz icing sugar, sifted
1 egg white	1 egg white
rice paper	rice paper

To decorate:

Metric	Imperial
glacé cherries	glacé cherries
crystallized angelica	crystallized angelica
crystallized pineapple	crystallized pineapple
blanched almond halves	blanched almond halves

To finish:

Metric	Imperial
2 × 5 ml spoons powdered gum arabic	2 teaspoons powdered gum arabic
2 × 15 ml spoons water	2 tablespoons water

Preparation time: 20 minutes, plus drying
Cooking time: 4–5 minutes
Oven: 230°C, 450°F, Gas Mark 8

Gum arabic is obtainable from chemists.

Mix the ground almonds and icing sugar together in a bowl. Add sufficient egg white to form a soft smooth paste.
Cover a baking sheet with rice paper. Put the mixture into a piping bag fitted with a large star nozzle and pipe small shapes on to the prepared sheet. Decorate with small pieces of glacé cherry, angelica, crystallized pineapple or blanched almond halves. Leave for several hours or overnight to dry.
Put the gum arabic and water into a bowl, standing over a bowl of hot water and allow to dissolve.
Place the biscuits in a preheated oven and bake for 4–5 minutes to brown the edges. Remove from the oven and immediately glaze with the gum arabic solution. Cool on a wire tray.
Keeps up to 4 weeks in an airtight tin.
Makes about 36

Almond leaves; Petits vacherins; Rout biscuits

Petits vacherins

Metric
120 g icing sugar, sifted
2 egg whites

Imperial
4½ oz icing sugar, sifted
2 egg whites

To finish:
250 ml double or
    whipping cream,
    whipped
225 g strawberries or
    other soft fruit

To finish:
8 fl oz double or
    whipping cream,
    whipped
8 oz strawberries or other
    soft fruit

Preparation time: 30 minutes
Cooking time: 1½–2 hours
Oven: 150°C, 300°F, Gas Mark 2

Put the icing sugar and egg whites into a large bowl,
standing over a saucepan of hot water. Whisk until the
mixture becomes thick and shiny and stands in stiff
peaks. Remove from the heat and beat until cool.
Place the meringue mixture into a piping bag fitted
with a small star nozzle. Pipe small nests no more than
4 cm/1½ inches in diameter on to silicone paper lined
baking sheets. Place in a preheated oven and bake for
1½–2 hours until dry, firm and easily lifted off the
paper. Cool on a wire tray.
Place the whipped cream in a piping bag fitted with a
small star nozzle and pipe a swirl of cream into the
centre of each vacherin. Top with a small strawberry
or half a larger one.
Meringue cases keep up to 3 weeks in an airtight tin.
When filled, eat on the same day.
Makes 20

CONFECTIONERY

Sweets are fun to prepare and make excellent presents too. Some of the simple recipes like Coffee Walnut Creams and Chocolate Nut Clusters can be made by the younger members of the family. Older ones may like to make Treacle Toffee or Fudge, but do make certain that sugar boiling is well supervised. Sugar reaches high temperatures when it boils, and can cause severe burns if not handled with care. If you like making sweets, keep a packet of powdered glucose and some chocolate in stock. Most of the other ingredients will probably be found in the storecupboard.

Coffee walnut creams

Metric	*Imperial*
450 g icing sugar	*1 lb icing sugar*
1 × 1.25 ml spoon cream of tartar	*¼ teaspoon cream of tartar*
2 × 5 ml spoons instant coffee	*2 teaspoons instant coffee*
1 × 15 ml spoon boiling water	*1 tablespoon boiling water*
2 × 15 ml spoons evaporated milk	*2 tablespoons evaporated milk*
walnut halves	*walnut halves*

Preparation time: 30 minutes

Sift the icing sugar and cream of tartar into a bowl. Dissolve the instant coffee in the boiling water and add to the sugar with the evaporated milk. Knead well until smooth, adding a little more water and sugar if necessary.
Roll out to 5 mm/¼ inch thickness on a board lightly dusted with icing sugar and cut into 2.5 cm/1 inch circles. Press half a walnut into the centre of each. Place on waxed or non-stick silicone paper on a flat surface and leave overnight to dry. Place in paper cases to serve.
Keeps up to 4 weeks in an airtight tin.
Makes 450 g/1 lb

Crystallized mint leaves; Peppermint creams; Chocolate peppermint creams; Coffee walnut creams

Peppermint creams

Metric	Imperial
450 g icing sugar	1 lb icing sugar
1 × 1.25 ml spoon cream of tartar	¼ teaspoon cream of tartar
2 × 15 ml spoons evaporated milk	2 tablespoons evaporated milk
1½ × 5 ml spoons peppermint flavouring or 1 × 2.5 ml spoon essence of peppermint	1½ teaspoons peppermint flavouring or ½ teaspoon essence of peppermint
½ egg white	½ egg white
green food colouring (optional)	green food colouring (optional)

Preparation time: 30 minutes

Sift the icing sugar and cream of tartar into a bowl. Add the evaporated milk, peppermint flavouring or essence and egg white. Knead to a pliable paste. If necessary add a little more egg white, but keep the paste firm enough to roll out.
Peppermint creams look very attractive if coloured pale green, or you may prefer to colour half the mixture and leave the rest white.
The easiest way to add colour is to dip the tip of a skewer into the food colouring and transfer a very small amount to the paste. Knead it in well on a board lightly dusted with icing sugar. Add more colour if necessary until the paste is coloured a delicate green. Roll out to 5 mm/¼ inch thickness and cut into 2.5 cm/1 inch circles. Place on waxed or non-stick silicone paper on a flat surface and leave for 24 hours to dry.
Keeps up to 4 weeks in an airtight tin.
Makes 450 g/1 lb

Chocolate peppermint creams

Metric	Imperial
100 g plain chocolate, broken in pieces	4 oz plain chocolate, broken in pieces
1 quantity Peppermint Creams (left)	1 quantity Peppermint Creams (left)
To decorate:	**To decorate:**
crystallized mint leaves (below)	crystallized mint leaves (below)
crystallized violets	crystallized violets

Preparation time: 20 minutes

Crystallized mint leaves look best with green tinted peppermint creams and crystallized violets on the white ones.

Place the chocolate pieces in a bowl over a pan of hot, but not boiling, water. When the chocolate has melted, dip half of each peppermint cream into the chocolate, then allow to drain for a second or two against the side of the bowl.
Place the coated peppermint creams on waxed or non-stick silicone paper to set and put a small crystallized mint leaf or a small piece of crystallized violet in the centre of each cream before the chocolate sets.
Keeps up to 4 weeks in an airtight tin.
Makes 500 g/1¼ lb

Crystallized mint leaves

Metric	Imperial
little egg white	little egg white
small mint leaves	small mint leaves
25–50 g caster sugar	1–2 oz caster sugar

Preparation time: 15 minutes

Make the crystallized mint leaves the day before they are to be used so that there is time for them to dry. Common mint, spearmint, or one of the other varieties such as ginger mint can be used. Choose the very small leaves near the top of the stem.

Put the egg white on a plate and beat lightly with a fork. Using a small paint brush, coat both sides of each leaf with the egg white, then toss in the sugar so that it is lightly covered. Place on waxed or non-stick silicone paper and leave to dry.
Keeps for 1 day.

Rum truffles (1)

Metric	Imperial
225 g plain chocolate, broken in pieces	8 oz plain chocolate, broken in pieces
100 ml double or whipping cream	3½ fl oz double or whipping cream
1 × 15 ml spoon rum	1 tablespoon rum
50 g chocolate vermicelli	2 oz chocolate vermicelli

Preparation time: 20 minutes, plus chilling

Rum truffles can be served as petits fours with after-dinner coffee.

Place the chocolate pieces in a bowl over a pan of warm water. Allow the chocolate to melt slowly without boiling the water. Bring the cream to the boil in a small pan, then cool until lukewarm.

Add the rum to the melted chocolate, remove from the heat and stir well. Stir in the cream and mix well together. Allow to cool until about 13°C/55°F. Beat well (use an electric mixer if possible) until the mixture becomes creamy and light in colour and texture. Leave to set in a cool place or for a brief time only in the refrigerator.

Put the chocolate vermicelli on a piece of greaseproof paper. When the truffle mixture is firm enough to handle, use 2 teaspoons to divide into about 30 pieces – these will be slightly sticky. Roll each one in the chocolate vermicelli until coated all over and a neat round shape.

Chill in the refrigerator until firm. Place in paper cases to serve.

Keeps up to 2 weeks in an airtight tin.

Makes about 30

Variations:
Use 50 g/2 oz cocoa or drinking chocolate powder to coat the truffles instead of chocolate vermicelli.

Brandy truffles: Substitute brandy for rum.

Coffee truffles: Substitute the rum with 1 × 15 ml spoon/1 tablespoon strong coffee essence made using 2 × 5 ml spoons/2 teaspoons instant coffee powder dissolved in 1 × 15 ml spoon/1 tablespoon boiling water.

Orange truffles: Add 1 × 15 ml spoon/1 tablespoon orange juice instead of rum. Add the finely grated rind of a small orange to the warmed cream.

Rum truffles (2)

Metric	Imperial
100 g Madeira or sponge cake crumbs	4 oz Madeira or sponge cake crumbs
75 g glacé fruits, finely chopped	3 oz glacé fruits, finely chopped
25 g mixed candied peel, finely chopped	1 oz mixed candied peel, finely chopped
1 × 15 ml spoon apricot jam	1 tablespoon apricot jam
1 × 15 ml spoon rum, or to taste	1 tablespoon rum, or to taste
50 g chocolate vermicelli	2 oz chocolate vermicelli

Preparation time: 20 minutes

These truffles are an ideal way of using leftover Madeira or sponge cake. They can be crumbled by hand, but will be finer and easier to mix evenly if the crumbs are made in a blender or food processor. If you do not want to make truffles immediately, the leftover crumbs can be frozen until needed. When made, the truffles may also be frozen. If cake or sponge crumbs are not available, crush sponge finger biscuits instead.

For an extra special flavour use a selection of glacé fruits, such as cherries, pineapple and a little ginger, but glacé cherries and angelica will be quite satisfactory.

Put the cake crumbs, chopped fruits and mixed peel into a bowl with the apricot jam. Add the rum to taste and mix well together.

Put the vermicelli on to a piece of greaseproof paper. Roll small spoonfuls of the truffle mixture in the vermicelli until they are coated and neat round shapes. Place in paper cases to serve.

Keeps up to 10 days in an airtight tin.

Makes 18–20

Rum truffles (1); Rum truffles (2); Stuffed dates

Stuffed dates

Preparation time: 30 minutes

Stuffed dates are quick to make and are popular served with coffee after a meal. They can also be put into boxes of homemade sweets where they make a delicious contrast to other sweets.

Metric	Imperial
175 g ready-made marzipan or 75 g ground almonds	*6 oz ready-made marzipan or 3 oz ground almonds*
1 × 5 ml spoon rum	*1 teaspoon rum*
green food colouring	*green food colouring*
75 g caster sugar	*3 oz caster sugar*
litle egg white	*little egg white*
1 box dates	*1 box dates*
icing sugar	*icing sugar*
granulated sugar, to finish	*granulated sugar, to finish*

If ready made marzipan is used, put in a bowl and mix with the rum and a drop or two of green food colouring, using a fork. Blend smoothly together.
Alternatively, to make the almond paste, put the ground almonds, sugar and rum in a bowl and add sufficient egg white to mix to a stiff paste. Blend in 1–2 drops green food colouring to colour the mixture to a soft apple green.
Slit along the top of each date and remove the stone. Sprinkle a pastry board or working surface with a little sifted icing sugar and roll the almond paste into a long sausage shape. Cut into as many pieces as there are dates. Shape each piece into a plump roll and use to replace the stone in each date. Roll in granulated sugar and place in paper cases to serve.
Keeps up to 4 weeks in an airtight tin.
Makes about 24

EASY CHOCOLATES

Chocolates are great favourites with everyone and many can be made easily at home. The type of chocolate you use is one of personal choice. A good dessert chocolate, either milk or plain has the best flavour but cooking chocolate, either in blocks or chips will melt easily and is cheaper to use. For the novice chocolate maker, practice with cooking chocolate first of all.

The following chocolate recipes are simple ones, just requiring the gentle melting of the chocolate, but even this needs care for a good result. Break the chocolate into small pieces and place in a bowl. Stand this over a pan of hot, but not boiling, water until the chocolate becomes liquid – this takes only 5–6 minutes. Take care that the water does not touch the bottom of the bowl and that the water does not boil. If chocolate becomes too hot, white streaks appear on the surface when it cools and these spoil the appearance of the finished chocolates.

Moisture or liquids will alter the texture of the chocolate and make it thick, so be careful that no water or steam touches the chocolate. The chocolates made at home by simply melting the chocolate will not have the high gloss of bought ones because of the different processes used in manufacture. Nonetheless, even with little or no experience you will soon be able to make some very attractive sweets.

Chocolate Brazils

Metric	Imperial
150 g chocolate	*6 oz chocolate*
100 g shelled Brazil nuts	*4 oz shelled Brazil nuts*

Preparation time: 20 minutes

Melt the chocolate carefully and, using 2 forks, carefully dip each Brazil nut into the chocolate, coating it completely. Allow any surplus chocolate to drain off against the side of the bowl before putting the nut on to a baking sheet lined with waxed or non-stick silicone paper.

Not all the chocolate can be used for dipping as it becomes too shallow. About 50 g/2 oz will be left in the bottom of the bowl, and this can be used to make a few Chocolate Nut Clusters (right).
Keeps up to 4 weeks in an airtight tin.
Makes about 225 g/8 oz

Variations:
Use blanched almonds in place of Brazil nuts.
Use glacé cherries or well drained and dried Maraschino cherries, stoned dates or raisins.
Use skinned hazelnuts and place them in clusters of 3 on the baking sheet.

Chocolate nut clusters

Metric	Imperial
225 g chocolate	*8 oz chocolate*
100 g nuts, chopped	*4 oz nuts, chopped*

Preparation time: 20 minutes
Cooking time: 10 minutes
Oven: 160°C, 325°F, Gas Mark 3

Almonds, hazelnuts, walnuts, unsalted cashew nuts or a mixture of any of these can be used. Ready chopped nuts or niblets are satisfactory and are ready to use. If you prefer hazelnuts and almonds to have a toasted flavour, put the chopped nuts on to a baking sheet and place in a preheated oven until they are golden brown. If they become too dark they will be rather bitter.

Melt the chocolate carefully, remove from the heat and add the chopped nuts. Stir until they are completely coated.
Test with a little of the mixture to see that it is firm enough to hold its shape when placed on a baking sheet lined with waxed or non-stick silicone paper. If it spreads, let the chocolate cool slightly before placing small spoonfuls on to the baking sheet. Leave to set and place in paper sweet cases to serve.
Keeps up to 4 weeks in an airtight tin.
Makes 18–20

Chocolate Brazils and variations; Chocolate nut clusters

Sugar boiling

When sugar is boiled, its character changes. First it becomes syrupy, then as the temperature rises, it gets thicker and sets to a soft consistency. The boiled sugar continues to change until it becomes a rich brown caramel which is hard and crisp when set. These changes are of immense importance to sweet makers, enabling them to make a large range of confectionery from soft fudge to chewy toffee or hard praline.

Because each change happens at a certain temperature, it is possible to get good results even without using a sugar thermometer, although, of course, it is a useful piece of equipment to buy if a lot of sugar boiling is planned. Choose a thermometer which is clearly marked. A large handle at the top makes it easy to move and a clip on the side ensures it stands upright in the pan and makes it easier to take an accurate reading.

UTENSILS

Choice of pan It is essential when boiling sugar to use a pan with a heavy base, thin ones will distort with the extreme heat. Aluminium and stainless steel are excellent, or you may be lucky enough to own a copper sugar boiling pan. These copper pans are not tinned as the tinning would melt in the temperatures reached and so it is most important that they *must not* be used for any cooking other than boiling sugar. Enamel pans are not suitable and non-stick pans should not be used for making fudge as the sugar grains will scratch the lining.

Spoons Always use wooden spoons or spatulas. Metal spoons will scratch the pan and if the handles are metal, they can become very hot and cause burns. Plastic ones will melt.

Tins For most recipes an 18 cm/7 inch square tin is ideal. Where other sizes are given, they have been found to be the best when the recipes were tested. Always place the tin on a board or pot stand. The temperatures reached in sweet making can damage plastic laminate working surfaces.

Asbestos sheet or a heat diffuser These can be a great help on a gas cooker when long slow cooking is needed.

INGREDIENTS

Sugar Unless stated otherwise, use granulated sugar.

Glucose This is used to prevent crystals forming in the sugar syrup. It can be bought as a thick colourless liquid or in powder form which is cheaper to buy and easier to weigh. Both types of glucose can be bought in chemists. Powdered glucose can also be bought at health food stores. Both will keep well in a cool dry larder.

Cream of tartar or tartaric acid This is also used in some recipes to prevent crystallization. Because it is so strong, only a small amount is needed. It can be bought from a chemist shop.

Butter This will give a better flavour than margarine.

FLAVOURINGS

Peppermint Oil of peppermint is strong and only a few drops are needed. It has become so expensive that it is not easy to buy, so the recipes in this book use peppermint essence or peppermint flavouring. Essence of peppermint is about 25 per cent of the strength of oil of peppermint. It is sold in small bottles. Peppermint flavouring is sometimes called peppermint flavouring essence, which can cause confusion, but it comes in larger 27 ml/1 fl oz bottles and is much cheaper to buy. It is not as strong as essence of peppermint.

Rose water and orange flower water These are used for flavouring and can also be purchased from a chemist shop. The quantities given in these recipes are for standard strength. Check the label before using as it is possible to buy triple strength and this will need diluting.

FOR SUCCESSFUL SUGAR BOILING

1. Prepare all tins etc., before starting to boil the sugar.
2. Use a perfectly clean pan.
3. Keep a small pan of water boiling on top of the cooker and keep the thermometer and spoons in this when they are not being used.
4. Allow the sugar to dissolve slowly, stirring gently if necessary.
5. Make certain that all the sugar has dissolved before the syrup comes to the boil.
6. Never stir a boiling syrup unless a recipe states otherwise.
7. Wash any sugar crystals from the side of the pan with a clean pastry brush dipped into water.
8. Remove any scum which forms on the top of the syrup with a metal spoon.
9. Cook over a moderate heat unless told to cook gently.
10. Have patience. Sugar sometimes takes a long time to rise from one temperature to another and will then rise very rapidly indeed. When the correct temperature is reached, remove the pan from the heat immediately.

USE AND CARE OF A SUGAR THERMOMETER

Always keep a pan of boiling water on top of the cooker and place the thermometer in this before and after it is used in the syrup.

Make certain that the syrup always covers the bulb of mercury.

Stand the thermometer upright in the pan and bend down so that the reading is taken at eye level.

After use, replace the thermometer in the pan of boiling water until it is clean, then rinse carefully in hot water and dry well. To store safely when not in use, keep it in a box in a drawer.

To clean the pan afterwards Allow the pan to cool, then fill with warm water. Cover with a lid and boil until all the sugar has dissolved.

STAGES OF SUGAR BOILING

The temperature at which sugar reaches each stage can be affected by altitude, atmosphere and even different bags of sugar can react differently. For accuracy the full range of temperatures are stated, but for general use a quick guide is also given.

Thread 107°C/225°F. The sugar looks syrupy. Using a small spoon remove a little of the syrup and allow it to fall from the spoon, on to a dish. The syrup should form a fine thin thread when the correct stage has been reached. Used in Crème au Beurre Mousseline.

Soft Ball 113–118°C/235–245°F. Drop a small amount of the syrup into cold water then mould into a soft ball with the fingers. Used for Fudge.

Hard Ball 119–127°C/246–260°F. Drop a little syrup into cold water, then using the fingers, mould into a ball which is firm but pliable. Used for Caramels and Marshmallows.

Small Crack 132–137°C/270–279°F. Drop a little syrup into cold water, it should set hard, but will bend slightly and stick to the teeth when bitten. Used for toffees.

Hard Crack 138–153°C/280–305°F. The syrup dropped into cold water will form brittle threads which snap easily. Used for hard toffee.

Caramel 154°C/310°F. The syrup becomes a light golden brown. As the temperature rises it gets darker in colour. If it becomes too dark, the flavour is bitter. When it is almost black it can be used as gravy browning.

QUICK TEMPERATURE GUIDE

Thread	107°C	225°F
Soft Ball	115°C	238°F
Hard Ball	121°C	250°F
Small Crack	132°C	270°F
Hard Crack	143°C	289°F
Caramel	154°C	310°F

Some equipment and ingredients needed for sugar boiling

Marzipan

Marzipan sweets are suitable for the beginner to try. An uncooked marzipan is easy to make but, like bought marzipan, tends to oil and crack if over-handled. The cooked marzipan needs more care in preparation but is easy and pliable to handle. If you want to add a touch of luxury, blend a little rum, brandy or liqueur into the paste.

Uncooked marzipan

Metric	Imperial
100 g icing sugar, sifted	4 oz icing sugar, sifted
100 g ground almonds	4 oz ground almonds
2 × 5 ml spoons lemon juice	2 teaspoons lemon juice
1 egg white	1 egg white

Preparation time: 10 minutes

Mix the icing sugar and ground almonds together in a bowl. Add the lemon juice and egg white and mix to a paste. Knead lightly until smooth. Keep tightly covered in a polythene box or bag until required. Use within 7 days.
Makes 225 g/8 oz

Cooked marzipan

Metric	Imperial
225 g sugar	8 oz sugar
6 × 15 ml spoons water	6 tablespoons water
175 g ground almonds	6 oz ground almonds
50 g liquid glucose	2 oz liquid glucose
1 egg white	1 egg white
1 × 5 ml spoon lemon juice	1 teaspoon lemon juice
225 g icing sugar, sifted	8 oz icing sugar, sifted

Preparation time: 15 minutes
Cooking time: 25 minutes

Put the sugar and water into a saucepan and stir over a low heat until dissolved, then stop stirring and boil until soft ball stage 115°C/238°F is reached.
Remove from the heat, stir in the ground almonds and glucose. Cool slightly, then add the egg white. Return to a gentle heat and cook, stirring all the time, for 2–3 minutes. Add the lemon juice.
Knead the mixture well while it is cooling, either on a board or in an electric mixer using a dough hook, working in sufficient icing sugar to give a firm but pliable consistency. Keep tightly covered in a polythene bag until required. Use within 7 days.
Makes about 750 g/1½ lb

Marzipan cherries

Metric	Imperial
100 g marzipan (left)	4 oz marzipan (left)
icing sugar	icing sugar
16–18 glacé or	16–18 glacé or
Maraschino cherries	Maraschino cherries

Preparation time: 15 minutes

Roll out the marzipan thinly on a board covered with a little sifted icing sugar. Cut into strips about 6 × 1 cm/2½ × ½ inch wide.
Wash the cherries and dry them well. Wrap a strip of marzipan around each cherry.
Keeps up to 4 weeks loosely covered.
Makes 16–18

Marzipan squares

Metric	Imperial
225 g marzipan (left)	8 oz marzipan (left)
green and red food	green and red food
colouring	colouring
icing sugar	icing sugar
little egg white	little egg white

Preparation time: 30 minutes

Divide the marzipan into 2, leave 1 part un-coloured. Colour half the remaining portion green and the other half colour red.
Make each colour into long bars 2.5 cm/1 inch thick; cut into 2 lengthwise. Brush them lightly with egg white and form into one block with the colours in opposite corners.
On a board dredged with sifted icing sugar, roll out the uncoloured marzipan thinly to a strip 10 cm/4 inches wide. Brush lightly with egg white and wrap around the outside of the coloured block. Cut into 1 cm/½ inch squares and seal the join neatly. Place in paper cases to serve.
Keeps up to 4 weeks loosely covered.
Makes about 20

Variation:
Dip the base of each into melted chocolate and leave to set on waxed or non-stick silicone paper.

From the top: Marzipan cherries; Marzipan fruits; Marzipan squares

Marzipan fruits

Metric	*Imperial*
225 g marzipan	8 oz marzipan
yellow, red, green, orange, brown and mauve food colouring	yellow, red, green, orange, brown and mauve food colouring
few cloves	few cloves
small strip of crystallized angelica	small strip of crystallized angelica
2 × 5 ml spoons caster sugar	2 teaspoons caster sugar

Preparation time: 30 minutes

With a little practice, you will soon find marzipan fruits easy to mould. If you intend to make a lot, it is well worth sparing the time to make a sago board to make the pitted skins of lemons, oranges and strawberries. To do this, spread a thin layer of glue on to a thin piece of hardboard. Sprinkle well with fine sago and shake off any surplus. Leave to dry. Once you have made a board, store it in a polythene bag and it will last a lifetime. Otherwise use a fine grater.

To make marzipan fruits, divide the mixture into 3 portions. Colour 1 portion yellow. Divide two-thirds into 4 and colour them red, green, mauve and orange. Remember to keep the marzipan in a polythene bag when not in use, as it will soon dry on the surface, crack and become difficult to handle.

To mould, each piece should weigh slightly less than 15 g/$\frac{1}{2}$ oz. 25 g/1 oz will make 3 pieces.

Lemons (yellow): Form into an egg shape, pinch the ends and roll against a fine grater or sago board.

Plums (mauve): Form into balls. Hold the ball against the back of a small vegetable knife and roll the knife back to make an indentation or crease on one side of the plum. Roll each one in caster sugar. Use a clove or small piece of angelica for a stalk.

Bananas (yellow): Form into a 4 sided bar about 3 cm/$1\frac{1}{4}$ inches long. Point each end and slightly curve the bar until it resembles a banana shape. Using a very fine paint brush and a little brown food colouring, paint soft lines along the square edges.

Strawberries (red): Make a ball, then work one end with the finger and thumb to make a strawberry shape. Roll against a sago board or fine grater. Use a small piece of angelica for a stalk.

Oranges (orange): Form into a ball. Roll against a sago board or fine grater. Use cloves for the stalk and calyx.

Keeps up to 4 weeks loosely covered.

Apples (green): Form into balls. 'Blush' with red food colouring and press cloves into each end to simulate the calyx and the stalk.

Makes 20

Fudge

Metric	Imperial
175 g condensed milk	6 oz condensed milk
50 g butter	2 oz butter
175 g brown sugar	6 oz brown sugar
50 g sugar	2 oz sugar
100 g powdered glucose	4 oz powdered glucose
120 ml water	4 fl oz water
few drops of vanilla essence	few drops of vanilla essence

Preparation time: 15 minutes
Cooking time: 30 minutes

Put the condensed milk and butter in a bowl over a pan of hot water and heat until melted. Put the brown and granulated sugars, powdered glucose and water in a medium pan and heat, stirring frequently, until dissolved. Continue to boil, without stirring until soft ball stage is reached (page 73) 115°C/238°F.
Pour in the warmed condensed milk and butter mixture, and stir well with a wooden spoon. Return the pan to the heat and stir well until it reheats to the same soft ball temperature. Dip the base of the pan briefly into cold water to stop it heating further, then stir until the mixture thickens to a creamy pouring consistency. Pour into an 18 cm/7 inch square tin lined on the base and sides with oiled greaseproof paper or nonstick silicone paper. Leave to set. When almost firm, mark into squares using an oiled knife. Cut when completely cold.
Keeps up to 4 weeks in an airtight tin.
Makes 450 g/1 lb

Variation:
Chocolate fudge: Melt 100 g/4 oz plain chocolate with the condensed milk and butter.

Coconut ice

Metric	Imperial
450 g sugar	1 lb sugar
150 ml water	$\frac{1}{4}$ pint water
150 g desiccated coconut	5 oz desiccated coconut
drop of red food colouring	drop of red food colouring

Preparation time: 15 minutes
Cooking time: 30 minutes

Put the sugar in a fairly large saucepan with the water, heat and stir frequently until the sugar has dissolved. Bring to the boil without stirring, and allow to boil steadily until soft ball stage 115°C/238°F is reached; when a teaspoon of the syrup dropped into a bowl of cold water will form a soft ball.
Add the coconut to the syrup and reboil to 119°C/246°F. At this stage a little syrup dropped into cold water will form a firm ball.
Pour half of the mixture into an 18 cm/7 inch square tin lined with non-stick silicone paper. Add a drop of red food colouring to the remainder and keep this soft by standing the saucepan in a larger pan of hot water. When the white layer is sufficiently set, cover with the pink coconut ice and smooth level. Leave to set until completely cold, then turn out and cut into 8 bars or individual squares.
Keeps up to 4 weeks in an airtight tin.
Makes 500 g/1$\frac{1}{4}$ lb

Turkish delight

Metric	Imperial
300 ml water	½ pint water
25 g powdered gelatine	1 oz powdered gelatine
450 g sugar	1 lb sugar
pink food colouring	pink food colouring
few drops of rose water	few drops of rose water

To finish:

2 × 15 ml spoons icing sugar, sifted	2 tablespoons icing sugar, sifted
2 × 15 ml spoons cornflour, sifted	2 tablespoons cornflour, sifted

Preparation time: 10 minutes
Cooking time: 30 minutes

Pour about one third of the water into a bowl and add the gelatine. Leave to soak. Meanwhile, put the rest of the water in a pan with the sugar. Place over a gentle heat and stir until the sugar has dissolved, then boil without stirring until soft ball stage 115°C/238°F is reached.

Remove from the heat and pour on to the gelatine. Stir well until the gelatine and the thick syrup are dissolved, then add a little pink food colouring. Return the syrup to the pan and boil without stirring, to the thread stage 107°C/225°F. Remove the pan from the heat.

Add a few drops of rose water, then take a small spoonful of the syrup from the pan and allow to cool before tasting. Add more rose water if necessary and pour the syrup into an 18 cm/7 inch square tin lined with non-stick silicone paper. Cool and set.

Mix the icing sugar and cornflour together and spread on a board. Turn out the Turkish delight and remove the silicone paper. Cut into squares and toss until completely coated in the sugar and cornflour.

Keeps up to 4 weeks in an airtight container.

Makes 500 g/1¼ lb

Nougat

Metric	Imperial
100 g blanched almonds, sliced into 2 or 3	4 oz blanched almonds, sliced into 2 or 3
15 g pistachio nuts, blanched and halved (optional)	½ oz pistachio nuts, blanched and halved (optional)
150 g icing sugar, sifted	5 oz icing sugar, sifted
100 g honey	4 oz honey
25 g powdered glucose	1 oz powdered glucose
2 egg whites	2 egg whites
50 g glacé cherries, sliced	2 oz glacé cherries, sliced
4 × 15 ml spoons sifted icing sugar	4 tablespoons sifted icing sugar
3 sheets rice paper	3 sheets rice paper

Preparation time: 15 minutes
Cooking time: 20 minutes
Oven: 160°C, 325°F, Gas Mark 3

Spread the almonds and pistachio nuts, if used, on a baking sheet. Place in a preheated oven to dry, then reduce the heat to keep them warm.

Put the icing sugar, honey, glucose and egg whites into a fairly large saucepan with a thick base, pre-ferably one with curved sides where it joins the base – a large milk saucepan is ideal. Place over a gentle heat and beat well until a little of the mixture, dropped into cold water forms a firm, but not hard, ball. This will take about 20 minutes. An electric hand whisk can be used at high speed until the mixture thickens, then reduce to medium speed; or beat with a large wooden spoon.

Add the warm nuts and the cherries. Mix well and turn out on to a board covered with the sifted icing sugar. Press out flat, about the size of an 18 cm/7 inch square tin. Place in the tin, lined on the bottom and sides with the rice paper, and flatten it even.

Cover with rice paper and place a piece of cardboard cut to shape or another tin of the same size over. Weigh down – a bag of sugar or a large can of fruit is about the right weight. Leave to cool, then cut into small bars or squares and wrap each in rice paper or waxed paper.

Keeps up to 4 weeks in an airtight tin.

Makes about 450 g/1 lb

Fudge; Coconut ice; Turkish delight; Nougat

Butterscotch; Treacle toffee; Creamy caramels; Toffee apples

Butterscotch

Metric	*Imperial*
225 g sugar	*8 oz sugar*
75 g powdered glucose	*3 oz powdered glucose*
150 ml water	*$\frac{1}{4}$ pint water*
50 g unsalted butter	*2 oz unsalted butter*

Preparation time: 10 minutes
Cooking time: 15 minutes

Put the sugar and powdered glucose into a saucepan with the water and bring to the boil, stirring frequently. When the sugar has dissolved, stop stirring and allow to heat steadily until hard crack stage 143°C/289°F is reached. Cut the butter into small pieces and stir into the hot syrup so that it colours slightly.
Pour into an oiled 18 cm/7 inch square tin. When the butterscotch has cooled sufficiently, mark into sections using an oiled knife. Break into pieces when cold.
Keeps up to 4 weeks in an airtight tin.
Makes 350 g/12 oz

Treacle toffee

Metric	*Imperial*
450 g soft brown sugar	*1 lb soft brown sugar*
150 ml water	*$\frac{1}{4}$ pint water*
150 g black treacle	*6 oz black treacle*
50 g butter	*2 oz butter*
2 × 15 ml spoons lemon juice	*2 tablespoons lemon juice*

Preparation time: 10 minutes
Cooking time: 30 minutes

Dissolve the sugar in the water in a heavy-based saucepan, then add the treacle and butter. Bring to the boil and boil until hard crack stage 143°C/289°F is reached.
Remove from the heat and add the lemon juice. Leave for a few seconds until the bubbling subsides then pour into a well greased 18 cm/7 inch square tin.
When the toffee has cooled sufficiently, mark into squares with a knife. Break into pieces when completely cold.
Keeps up to 4 weeks in an airtight tin.
Makes 750 g/1$\frac{1}{2}$ lb

Creamy caramels

Metric	Imperial
350 g sugar	12 oz sugar
175 g powdered glucose	6 oz powdered glucose
1 × 175 g can evaporated milk	1 × 6 oz can evaporated milk
100 ml single cream	3½ fl oz single cream
few drops of vanilla essence	few drops of vanilla essence

Preparation time: 10 minutes
Cooking time: 50–60 minutes

Put the sugar, glucose, evaporated milk and cream into a saucepan and let the sugar dissolve slowly, stirring constantly. Bring the syrup to the boil and cook over a very low heat, stirring gently, until hard ball stage 121°C/250°F is reached. An asbestos mat or a heat diffuser will help to prevent the toffee burning on the bottom of the pan.
If the mixture appears to curdle or separate, give it a good brisk stir before pouring it into a buttered 18 cm/7 inch square tin placed on a board.
When almost set, mark into squares and break into pieces when completely cold.
Keeps up to 2 weeks in an airtight tin.
Makes 500 g/1¼ lb

Toffee apples

Metric	Imperial
8–9 medium dessert apples	8–9 medium dessert apples
8–9 wooden skewers or lolly sticks	8–9 wooden skewers or lolly sticks
450 g demerara sugar	1 lb demerara sugar
50 g powdered glucose	2 oz powdered glucose
1 × 15 ml spoon golden syrup	1 tablespoon golden syrup
2 × 5 ml spoons vinegar	2 teaspoons vinegar
150 ml water	¼ pint water
50 g butter	2 oz butter

Preparation time: 10 minutes
Cooking time: 25 minutes

Wash the apples, dry them well and push the sticks into the cores.
Put all the remaining ingredients into a medium heavy-based saucepan and place over a gentle heat. Stir until the sugar has dissolved, then bring to the boil and boil rapidly without stirring until hard crack stage 143°C/289°F is reached.
Dip the apples into the toffee. Allow the excess toffee to drip off for a few seconds and then dip again if the coating is thin. Leave on a baking sheet covered with waxed paper for 10–15 minutes until cold.
Keeps up to 7 days in a dry place, wrapped in waxed paper or cling film.
Makes 8–9

INDEX

Aigrettes au fromage 44
Almond:
  Almond dartois 34
  Almond leaves 64
  Conversations 34
  Praline 21
  Ratafias 63
  Rout biscuits 64
  Tarte frangipane 16
Anchovy canapés 42
Apple:
  Apple and apricot strudel 15
  Apple and date slices 28
  Apple and orange flan 47
  Gâteau jalousie aux pommes 22
  Tarte de pommes à la normande 22
  Toffee apples 79
Apricot:
  Apple and apricot strudel 15
  Apricot meringue 54
  Tarte aux abricots bourdaloue 16

Bacon:
  York fingers 38
Barquettes aux crevettes 37
Blackcurrant:
  Canelle tartelettes 33
Blue cheese canapés 43
Bouchées 37
Brandy truffles 68
Butterscotch 78
Butterscotch pear flan 52

Canapés 42–3
Canelle tartelettes 33
Caribbean flan 48
Cheese:
  Aigrettes au fromage 44
  Blue cheese canapés 43
  Cheese dartois 44
  Cheese palmiers 39
  Cheese pastry 7
  Cheese straws 38
  Nutty cheese bites 39
  Savoury cornets 44
  Spicy cheese canapés 43
Cherry:
  Marzipan cherries 74
  Tarte aux cerises alsacienne 18
Chestnut boats 32
Chocolate:
  Chocolate balls 62
  Chocolate boxes 57
  Chocolate Brazils 71
  Chocolate éclairs 30
  Chocolate fudge 76
  Chocolate nut clusters 71
  Chocolate peppermint creams 67
  Chocolate and rum tartlets 33
Choux aux fraises 24
Choux pastry 10
Coconut ice 76
Coconut slices 26
Coffee:
  Coffee chiffon pie 52
  Coffee truffles 68
  Coffee walnut creams 66
Confectioner's custard 13
Confectionery see Sweets
Continental pastries:
  Apple and apricot strudel 15
  Choux aux fraises 24
  Gâteau jalousie aux pommes 22
  Gâteau Saint Honoré 19
  Linzer torte 14
  Paris-Brest 20
  Polkas 21
  Tarte aux abricots bourdaloue 16

Tarte aux cerises alsacienne 18
Tarte frangipane 16
Tarte de pommes à la normande 22
Tarte aux raisins 17
Tartelettes aux fruits 13
Tranche aux fruits 24
Conversations 34
Coventry godcakes 28
Cream horns 31
Creamy caramels 79
Crème au beurre mousseline 57
Crème patissière 13
Crystallized mint leaves 67

Damson puff pie 48
Danish cream tarts 31
Date:
  Apple and date slices 28
  Stuffed dates 69
Doigts des dames 63

Eccles cakes 28

Flaky pastry 8
Flans see Tarts and flans
Friandises 58
Fruit. See also Apple etc.
  Marzipan fruits 75
  Tartelettes aux fruits 13
Fudge 76

Gâteau jalousie aux pommes 22
Gâteau Saint Honoré 19
Genoese sponge 56
Grape:
  Tarte aux raisins 17

Iced walnut squares 61
Italiens 58

Langues de chat à la crème 62
Linzer torte 14

Marzipan sweets 74–5
Mint leaves, crystallized 67
Moka fudge flan 53

Nougat 77
Nutty cheese bites 39

Orange:
  Apple and orange flan 47
  Orange flower water 72
  Orange truffles 68

Palmiers 27
Paris-Brest 20
Pastry:
  To line a flan ring 6
  Cheese pastry 7
  Choux pastry 10
  Fault finding guide 11
  Flaky pastry 8
  Pâte brisée (rich shortcrust pastry) 7
  Pâte sucrée 8
  Puff pastry 9
  Shortcrust pastry 6
  Wholemeal shortcrust pastry 6
Pâte brisée 7
Pâte sucrée 8
Peach flan 47
Pear:
  Butterscotch pear flan 52
  Tarte aux poires au vin rouge 55
Peppermint creams 67
Peppermint flavouring 72
Petits choux 40

Petits fours 56–65
Petits vacherins 65
Pies. See also Tarts and flans
  Coffee chiffon pie 52
  Damson puff pie 48
Pineapple and cottage cheese flan 50
Pineapple tartlets 27
Polkas 21
Praline 21
Prawn:
  Barquettes aux crevettes 37
Printaniers 59
Puff pastry 9

Ratafias 63
Rose water 72
Rout biscuits 64
Rum truffles 68

Sacristans 35
Sardine crescents 40
Savoury cornets 44
Savoury pastries:
  Aigrettes au fromage 44
  Barquettes aux crevettes 37
  Bouchées 37
  Canapés 42–3
  Cheese dartois 44
  Cheese palmiers 39
  Cheese straws 38
  Nutty cheese bites 39
  Petits choux 40
  Sardine crescents 40
  Savoury cornets 44
  Talmouse of smoked haddock 41
  York fingers 38
Shortcrust pastry 6; rich (pâte brisée) 7
Smoked haddock, talmouse of 41
Spicy cheese canapés 43
Strawberry:
  Choux aux fraises 24
  Polkas 21
  Tranche aux fruits 24
Stuffed dates 69
Sweets:
  To boil sugar 72–3
  Brandy truffles 68
  Butterscotch 78
  Chocolate Brazils 71
  Chocolate nut clusters 71
  Chocolate peppermint creams 67
  Coconut ice 76
  Coffee truffles 68
  Coffee walnut creams 66
  Creamy caramels 79
  Crystallized mint leaves 67
  Fudge 76
  Marzipan sweets 74–5
  Nougat 77
  Orange truffles 68
  Peppermint creams 67
  Rum truffles 68
  Stuffed dates 69
  Toffee apples 79
  Treacle toffee 78
  Turkish delight 77

Talmouse of smoked haddock 41
Tarte aux abricots bourdaloue 16
Tarte aux cerises alsacienne 18
Tarte frangipane 16
Tarte aux poires au vin rouge 55
Tarte de pommes à la normande 22
Tarte aux raisins 17
Tartelettes aux fruits 13

Tarts, tartlets and flans:
  Apple and orange flan 47
  Apricot meringue 54
  Butterscotch pear flan 52
  Canelle tartelettes 33
  Caribbean flan 48
  Chestnut boats 32
  Chocolate and rum tartlets 33
  Conversations 34
  Danish cream tarts 31
  Moka fudge flan 53
  Peach flan 47
  Pineapple and cottage cheese flan 50
  Pineapple tartlets 27
  Tarte aux abricots bourdaloue 16
  Tarte aux cerises alsacienne 18
  Tarte frangipane 16
  Tarte aux poires au vin rouge 55
  Tarte de pommes à la normande 22
  Tarte aux raisins 17
  Tartelettes aux fruits 13
  Tranche aux fruits 24
  Treacle tart 50
  Yorkshire curd tart 51
Teatime pastries:
  Almond dartois 34
  Apple and date slices 28
  Canelle tartelettes 33
  Chestnut boats 32
  Chocolate éclairs 30
  Chocolate and rum tartlets 33
  Coconut slices 26
  Conversations 34
  Coventry godcakes 28
  Cream horns 31
  Danish cream tarts 31
  Eccles cakes 28
  Palmiers 27
  Pineapple tartlets 27
  Sacristans 35
  Toffee apples 79
  Tranche aux fruits 24
  Treacle tart 50
  Treacle toffee 78
  Tuiles aux noisettes 61
  Turkish delight 77

Viscontis 60

Walnut:
  Coffee walnut creams 66
  Iced walnut squares 61
Wholemeal shortcrust pastry 6

York fingers 38
Yorkshire curd tart 51

PDO 82-0421

ACKNOWLEDGEMENTS

The Publishers would like to thank the following company for their kindness
in providing backing equipment for photography:

Divertimenti, 139 Fulham Road, London W1.

The publishers would also like to thank:

The Tante Maric School of Cookery, Woodham House, Carlton Road,
Woking, Surrey.

Photographer Christine Hanscomb with stylist Antonia Gaunt

Home economists Linda Maclean and Carole Handslip